The Perfect Blend
Devotional

Daily Anecdotes and Biblical Inspiration for Successfully
Managing the Blended Family

Cathy L. Wray

WESTBOW
PRESS
A DIVISION OF THOMAS NELSON
& ZONDERVAN

Scripture taken from the King James Version of the Bible.

All Scripture quotations in this publications are from **The Message**.
Copyright (c) by Eugene H. Peterson 1993, 1994, 1995, 1996, 2000,
2001, 2002. Used by permission of NavPress Publishing Group.

WestBow Press books may be ordered through booksellers or by contacting:

WestBow Press
A Division of Thomas Nelson & Zondervan
1663 Liberty Drive
Bloomington, IN 47403
www.westbowpress.com
1 (866) 928-1240

ISBN: 978-1-4908-2124-5 (sc)
ISBN: 978-1-4908-2125-2 (e)

Library of Congress Control Number: 2014900294

Printed in the United States of America.

WestBow Press rev. date: 02/07/2014

Contents

Foreword

The Perfect Blend Devotional

Although I have helped to restore thousands of blended families from across the world, on occasion, a quiet voice whispers in my ear, "Your family isn't perfect." The enemy attempts to stifle our progress with subtle scare tactics, but then I remember that the Bible is full of blended families: Abraham, Sarah and Hagar; Elkanah, Hannah and Peninnah. Jesus, Himself, was raised by a man who was not His biological father. Despite the dysfunction, the families were blessed and great nations were created.

Throughout her book, *The Perfect Blend Devotional*, Cathy provides valuable insight, biblical principles and practical tools to eradicate the I-just-can't-seem-to-make-my-family-function excuses. With concise nuggets of wisdom and honest assessments gleaned from years of experience, she inspires you to transition your family from chaos to calm.

To effectively manage the dynamics of a blended family, wisdom is essential. Not only do you have to assess the true motive behind your actions, but you have to understand those of the children, your spouse and the other parent. Cathy encourages, empowers and motivates you to embody the wisdom noted in Scriptures like

A wise man learns from his own mistakes, an even wiser man learns from the mistakes of others. Proverbs 1:5; 9:9 (paraphrased) *"By wisdom a house is built, and through understanding it is established"* (Proverbs 24:3).

Life is a series of choices. You choose to do right or wrong. You choose to believe or doubt. You choose to succeed or fail. And by reading *The Perfect Blend Devotional*, you choose for your family to succeed.

Begin the journey of walking in your purpose to ensure the success of your family. The souls of the children are at stake.

-Valerie J. Lewis Coleman, multi award-winning author of *Blended Families an Anthology,* <u>**www.PenOfTheWriter.Com**</u>

Dedication

This book is dedicated to my wonderful husband who is the bedrock of our family and has provided the example and inspiration for every page. Without question you have modeled God's design for Leadership in the Blended Family as you raised our five beautiful children, none of who were biologically related to you. We came together from pieces and parts (three adopted and two from a previous marriage) and you managed to make our family seamless. You never backed down from your assignment and because of it our lives have been blessed beyond measure.

My hope and prayer is that every blended family -- every single mom, single dad, divorcee` or widower who will become a blended family one day -- will read this devotional and find the healing, help, encouragement and inspiration necessary to make their family The Perfect Blend.

"The proof that you love someone is not that you have warm affectionate feelings toward them. The proof is in your actions, your words and your sacrifice, your willingness to give the best of yourself and your willingness to get nothing in return."

- Katherine Walden

Introduction

Current research shows that 1 in 3 marriages in the United States will end in divorce. This is irrespective of whether it is a Christian marriage or not. 1/3 of all children in America will be born to a single mother; 50% of all first, 68% of all second, and 70% of all third marriages will end in divorce. 850,000 children are born out of wedlock in the U.S. each year and statisticians predict that ninety-five percent of all divorced, widowed or otherwise single persons will eventually remarry. This isn't a negative confession, but the truth is blended families will be around for some time to come.

Ecclesiastes states it well that, *"...there is nothing new under the sun..."* Blended families are not a new concept. Jacob had twelve children by two different women as is narrated in Genesis 35:22-26. I'd say that was certainly a blended family. Moses was a part of a blended family as is told in Exodus 2:10; Esther was a part of a blended family as is referenced in Esther 2:5; and even Jesus was a part of a blended family as is seen in Luke 2:41-48.

"God sets the solitary in families..."

~Psalm 68:6 (NKJV)

Though the existence of the blended family is a stark reality in our society, the Church is almost silent when it comes to addressing the unique marriage and parenting challenges that the blended family may face. One of the reasons I believe the church is quiet, is because we would then have to admit to the fact that divorce is happening in our churches in epidemic proportions, and it's happening from the pulpit to the pews.

Malachi 2:16 tells us in no uncertain terms, *"For the LORD, the God of Israel, saith that he hateth putting away..."* God hated divorce then, and He still hates divorce now. But, I believe that Jesus gave us more insight into the matter in Matthew 19:8 when He said, *"Moses **because of the hardness of your hearts** suffered you to put away your wives: but from the beginning it was not so."* Gary Thomas said it well, "People don't fall out of love; they fall out of forgiveness." Where ever there is pride and an unwillingness to forgive, the end result will be separation, tearing away, and falling apart. The hardness of one's heart...PRIDE...is what drives a wedge that is often irreparable. Proverbs 13:13 tells us, *"Only by pride cometh contention..."* Both my husband and I have experienced failed marriages so we are keenly aware of the pain associated with tearing away and falling apart. We both had to admit and come face-to-face with the pride and unforgiveness that drove us from our first marriages, before we could truly experience the success in marriage and in our family that we now enjoy.

One thing I love about God is that He is always in the restoration business. We may make decisions that cause us to experience brokenness in one way or another, but He is always working with and for us to put things back together again. God knew that our lives wouldn't always measure up to His ideals, yet He made provision for us. Psalm 68:6 tells us that it is God who sets the solitary into families.

Psalm 127:1 assures us that, no matter what the individual components are, only God can build the house. All of our other efforts apart from Him will be in vain. Look how God is right now building His own house with those of us who were not originally chosen, but are now adopted and grafted in. Everyone who believes in Jesus now has the right to become a child of God. We were the children of the Devil, but God made provision for us and called us His very own without any distinctions or restrictions. Adoption into a family places us sons, it preserves the family name, and continues the family's way of life. On top of all that, the adopted child now has an equal share in the inheritance right along with any natural son. Jesus Christ is the natural heir of all things based on His birth and perfect obedience. But, we've been adopted and made equal simply because we believe. *"But you have received the spirit of adoption as sons by which we cry out, 'Abba Father'."* – Romans 8:15.

The word 'build' in Psalm 127:1 is the Hebrew word *bana.* This word means to set, build, **rebuild**, establish, or cause to continue. When we look at the lineage of Jesus outlined in Luke 3:23, we see that Jesus had to be placed into a natural lineage so that we could have a spiritual lineage. He was placed as Joseph's son, which was in the lineage of Seth or the lineage of covenant. The name Seth actually means "placing" or "setting." God is no respecter persons. Just like Jesus, we have now been placed into God's family as sons. God trusted Joseph with Jesus, and when it comes to our blended families, He is trusting us to care for children we did not birth and to lead homes that may have been pieced together.

God is not the author of divorce or the perpetuator of loss but, I believe blended families can be purposely and strategically formed by God. When He is finished building the house, every gift, every talent, every personality, strength, and weakness of each family member can be used to give Him glory where the enemy intended for destruction.

The Perfect Blend Devotional offers biblical insight for the blended family. If you are not a Christian, I invite you to receive Jesus as your personal Lord and Savior. Following His way is the only thing that will guarantee you the help you need to make your new family a success.

Pray this prayer, mean it from your heart, and God can begin to do something brand new in you and in your family:

> *Father, I come to you in the name of Jesus. I acknowledge that I am a sinner and I need your forgiveness. I believe that Jesus Christ shed His precious blood on the cross at Calvary and died for my sins. You said in Your Holy Word, Romans 10:9 that if we confess the Lord our God and believe in our hearts that God raised Jesus from the dead, we shall be saved. Right now I confess Jesus as the Lord and I believe that God raised Jesus from the dead. This very moment I accept Jesus Christ as my own personal Savior and according to His Word, right now I am saved. Amen.*

I trust that The Perfect Blend Devotional will encourage you, enlighten you, and motivate you! You may have failed in your first marriage…I did. But, I found out that failure was not my final outcome. God had another plan for me and my children. And, just like everything that God does, this too is GOOD!

Laying the Proper Foundation

A solid building starts with a strong foundation; that part of structure that lies beneath what is initially visible to the eye. Any construction engineer will tell you that a foundation serves many purposes for a building: 1) to prevent settlement of the structure, 2) to allow refuge over water or water-logged ground, 3) to resist uplifting or overturning forces due to wind and elemental adversity, 4) to resist lateral forces due to soil movement, and 5) to reinforce unstable or previously existing structures. Normally, construction of any structure, be it a residence or a skyscraper; starts with the laying of foundations. The weight and height of a building will determine the depth of foundation that needs to be laid. The foundation of a structure is similar to the root system of a tree, without which the tree would not be able to stand.

What and how we think is the foundation for our marriage. It influences what we believe and what we say, and eventually leads to how we act. Consequently, how and what we think about each member

"God created marriage. No government subcommittee envisioned it. No social organization developed it. Marriage was conceived and born in the mind of God."

~ Max Lucado

of our blended family will have a tremendous impact on how solid this new family foundation will be. It is an established principle. Jesus was teaching the disciples about many such life principles in Luke chapter six. In chapter six, verse forty-eight He says this about laying a strong foundation:

"He is like a man which built an house, and digged deep, and laid the foundation on a rock: and when the flood arose, the stream beat vehemently upon that house, and could not shake it: for it was founded upon a rock. But he that heareth, and doeth not, is like a man that without a foundation built an house upon the earth; against which the stream did beat vehemently, and immediately it fell; and the ruin of that house was great."

Notice He says 'when' not 'if' the flood arose. In any relationship there will be tests and trials. In the blended family the stakes are much higher.

The number one cause for divorce in second marriages is disputes about the children. Satan's most successful tactic is to bring division and strife where God wants unity. Using terms like 'his kids', 'her kids', or 'step kids', rather than 'our kids' subtly diminishes our *love responsibilities* toward one another. Responsibilities that require: a) parents to love, care for and nurture anybody under their care, and b) children to honor, respect and obey the authority in the home (whether biological or not). Having a tight-knit blended family will only happen on purpose.

In Psalms 68:6, the scripture says that it is God who sets those who are alone into families. Trust me it doesn't surprised God that people may be widowed, divorced, or otherwise single and, I don't think He intends that life stops where you are today. Statistics show that 95% of all divorced or widowed people will eventually remarry. As a result, millions of people will face the challenge of blending two already existent families into one cohesive unit. Notice that the scripture says that God is the one who takes individuals and makes them into a family unit. Only He is able to take what most people would consider utter chaos and bring peace and unity. That is of course, if we will follow Proverbs 3:5-6, and acknowledge God for our next step. Whenever we try to do things on our own, or simply do nothing at all, is when we're destined to fail.

Before we can move forward successfully into a new relationship, we often must re-visit the past. If our previous marriages failed, we contributed something to the demise of the marriage whether directly or indirectly. There's usually the tendency to blame the other party, but we often don't own up to our contribution to the failure. Proverbs 21:2 says, *"Every way of man is right in his own eyes..."* So, even if you can claim no guilt, honestly examine your heart for pride, bitterness, and unforgiveness.

As we move forward, Leviticus 19:34 shows God's instruction on how to treat non-biological additions to the family. In the Old Testament, and quite frankly throughout scripture, it was common practice to accept people not born to you, into your family unit. Truth be told, according to today's vernacular, Jesus was a step-son to Joseph. Yet, in Luke 2:48 when his mother and Joseph found him in the temple after three days, Mary's first words to him were, "why have you done this...*your father* and I have been sorrowing for three days."

Matthew 12:25 plainly states that a house that is divided in any way will not stand. The term "step" as it relates to the family is not in the bible. "Step-parent" "step-family" and "step-child" are western civilization terms that delineate between biological and non-biological origin. Their underlying purpose simply lessens covenant responsibilities in families; parents toward the children, and children toward the parents. However, the composition of the family should never be allowed to change God's original design and intention for the family. God is a God of order, so it is no surprise that there is a specific design for the family.

Regardless of who the players are, the rules of the game remain the same. Ephesians 5:23 says, *"For the husband is the head of the wife, even as Christ is the head of the church: and he is the Savior of the body."* The husband should be the leader, the visionary, the forerunner in the family. He should provide leadership, vision, and mission. Proverbs 29:18 says, *"Where there is no vision, the people perish…"* Another version says, *"…the people cast off restraint."* Men, when you have a mission, it subconsciously sets your mind on course for where you're headed and programs you to accomplish it. Without a mission, you inadvertently tell your brain that you have no place to go and that anything will suffice.

I Timothy 5:14 says, *"…women should marry, bear children, guide the house, give none occasion to the adversary to speak reproachfully."* The wife should support, undergird, and manage the vision already given for the home. The wife must allow the husband to lead and then support his leadership.

When we deviate from God's plan, we open a door to the enemy to bring devastation. So, take the necessary steps to lay the proper foundation in your family:

o   Spend time together in prayer, asking God for direction for your family. What are some goals that you can set together? What kind of final product do you want to end up with? Get specific and begin to lay adequate prayer support.

o   Make a decision to truly embrace every member of your new family as your 'own' regardless of their biological origin. Make a plan to develop and maintain the proper mindset about each member of your new family.

o   Safeguard your family against Satan's attacks; eliminate terms like "step" "his kids" "her kids" and instead create terms of endearment toward one another that will strengthen and not diminish your love responsibilities.

o   If things are out of order today, begin today seeking wisdom from God's Word. Allow God to re-structure and rebuild your household so it represents His design for the family.

Let's Pray....

Father, I want your plan for my marriage. Give me the wisdom I need from your Word to set things in order. Teach me to stay in my role. Help me to have genuine care and concern for every person in our household. Cause our foundation to be established on the Rock and the principles of your Word. Amen.

Things to ponder:

1. How have you thought about the members in your blended family?

2. Have your thoughts had an impact on the family members in particular?

3. Was your family foundation laid according to God's original plan for the family?

4. Jot down three things that you can change immediately that will improve your blended family:

    a.

    b.

    c.

NOTES:

_____

_____

_____

_____

_____

_____

_____

_____

_____

_____

_____

_____

_____

_____

_____

_____

_____

_____

_____

_____

_____

_____

_____

_____

_____

_____

_____

_____

_____

Two Becoming One - The Power of Agreement

In geography, a confluence is the term used when there is a meeting of two or more bodies of water. Known also as a conflux, it refers either to the point where a tributary joins a larger river, called the main stem, or where two streams meet to become the source of a river of a new name, such as the confluence of the Monongahela and Allegheny Rivers in Pittsburgh, Pennsylvania creating the Ohio River.

The blended family is a conflux indeed...husband, wife, and children; all meeting together to become the source of one new name.

We've already established that it is God who makes 'oneness' into a family; but it is the job of the parents in the home to maintain that oneness. Often cracks in the marital foundation create opportunities for the entire family to become disjointed. A high level of commitment will be necessary from each marriage partner for the blended family to truly become one and to be a success.

"There is no more lovely, friendly or charming relationship, communion or company, than a good marriage."

~ Martin Luther

In Genesis 2:21-24 God commanded the man and the wife to leave the influence of their family and friends, and cleave, or stick to, one another. Their first responsibility was to work at meshing their thoughts, ideas, and desires so that their relationship became seamless. Outside influences were not permitted to take precedence over the decisions of the man and his wife in the home. Amos 3:3 asks this question, *"Can two walk together, except they be agreed?"* This doesn't mean that there will be agreement on every single point of every single matter, but as a couple there is a commitment to stay on course for the vision for the family, and to refuse to allow anything to drive you in opposing directions.

Ecclesiastes 4:9-12 talks about a three-fold cord and how it is not easily broken; in other words the husband, the wife, and God together are the majority against any obstacle. When a husband and wife have made the necessary commitment to the marriage and to the family, it will be very difficult for anything to come between them. But, keep in mind there is no such thing as instant unity. Since marriage and family is God's idea and design, we must continually strive to keep or maintain that unity...but it won't be automatic. In fact, Ephesians 4:3 tells us to, *"Endeavor to keep the unity of the Spirit in the bond of peace."* The word 'endeavor' here is the Greek word *spudazo*, and it means to exert oneself speedily and give all diligence toward the effort. I wonder if it's where we get the word *speedo* from? At any rate, the ultimate success of any team will depend on the individual commitment and full contribution from each player to perform their assigned tasks. In marriage, each partner must be willing to give 100%. In a blended family, the stakes are higher, so the commitment will need to be greater since statistics show that 67% of all second marriages will end in divorce.

Often very little thought is given to the power of agreement in marriage. In fact, in the story of the Tower of Babel, God said that nothing would be impossible because of agreement. II Corinthians 2:11 warns us, however, not to be ignorant of the trickeries that the enemy uses against us. He uses mental perceptions, evil thoughts and influences to take advantage of us and exert his plan for our demise. Don't fall for it! Know that the fight is not against your spouse, but against an unseen enemy who shows no mercy. Together you are unstoppable. Deuteronomy 32:30 declares, *"...one can chase a thousand, and two will put ten thousand to flight..."*

In the blended family some other factors that test our agreement will usually come in to play. Sometimes they will be subtle, and sometimes not. The same statistics that say 67% of second marriage end in divorce also say the primary reason for these divorces is directly related to disagreements about the children. Think about it, we will send our children to school, to coaches, and to other care providers and they must respect their authority and obey their rules. But, we will marry someone and tell them they cannot discipline 'my' kids. If you are the biological parent of a child brought into a blended family, you have a huge responsibility to facilitate agreement. You can do this by making sure that your spouse is respected and obeyed as an authority of that home no matter what. The children should see God's structure for the family modeled in your home regardless of the involvement, or lack of, from the other biological parent.

Let's look at some ways that two can become one:

o   As the biological parent of the children in the home, there are many ways that you can facilitate oneness in your family. Deciding to always have a united front is one of those things. Agree to disagree in private. Require your children to respect your spouse as an authority in the home at all times.

o   If you haven't done so already, revisit God's order for the home and make the provisions to re-order your family so that it lines up with God's plan.

o   Make sure all of the children involved understand what happens in this household. They may be subject to a different set of rules if they have visitation elsewhere, but make sure there is agreement in your house.

o   There are so many other things that can be done to increase family unity, such as: spending time together, developing hobbies that you participate in together, having family meetings, or going out to breakfast or dinner once a month as a family, just to name a few. In a nutshell, take an interest in each other's life, goals and dreams.

o   Prepare ahead of time for the task ahead of you. Decide that you are committed, no matter what happens…and trust me you'll have many opportunities to back out! Be honest with yourself about any areas you can personally improve in to make your marriage and family better.

Let's Pray…

Father, I repent for being in disunity with my spouse. I commit from today forward to get over onto the Word and to walk in agreement. I will train the children to honor you and to reverence any authority in the home. I refuse to allow any outside or inside influence to separate me from my spouse. Cause our marriage to become a powerful example of your plan for the family. Amen

Things to ponder:

1. Given that 67% of second marriages end in divorce, what are some steps you can take to ensure the success of your marriage and blended family?

2. If you are the biological parent in your home, what will you do based on what you have read, to ensure that your spouse is respected and obeyed?

3. A great family project can be to hear your family's thoughts on how to mke your blended become seamless.

NOTES:

_____
_____
_____
_____
_____
_____
_____
_____
_____
_____
_____
_____
_____
_____
_____
_____
_____
_____
_____
_____
_____
_____
_____
_____
_____
_____
_____
_____

Before You Say I Do

As a business professional by trade, I've learned there are five stages of successful business planning that are generally accepted in the industry: 1) Analysis – Where are we now, 2) Objective - Where we want to go, 3) Strategy – How will we get there, 4) Cost – What will it cost me, and 5) Commitment – What am I willing to give to make it happen. Luke 16:8 says "...*for the children of this world are in their generation wiser than the children of light.*" Even the secular business world understands how important it is to thoroughly assess any venture before jumping headlong into it.

The institution of marriage has evolved significantly over the last century. Today one in every three marriages, whether Christian or not, ends in divorce. One-third of all children born in the United States are born to a single mother. With that being said, it is highly likely that one considering marriage in the 21st century, will enter into that union as a blended family. Let's discuss some things to consider before saying "I do."

"What you are as a single person, you will be as a married person, only to a greater degree. Any negative character trait will be intensified in a marriage relationship, because you will feel free to let your guard down – that person has committed himself to you and you no longer have to worry about scaring him off."

– Josh McDowell

In Luke 14:25-35, Jesus is teaching on discipleship. He begins by telling his disciples to make sure they understand and agree to the commitment they are about to make in following Him because there would be no turning back. Likewise, every major decision in our lives should be preceded with counting up the costs…especially when entering into a blended family. There are a unique set of circumstances the blended family will encounter that the traditional family will never experience. Some of these circumstances include baby mamma/daddy drama, visitation and custody arrangements, payment of child support, acquisition of new debt, discipline of non-biological children, and on and on.

In Luke 9:23 Jesus makes it clear that it will take much patience and sacrifice to live the Christian life. Similarly, there is no such thing as the fairy tale blended family either. Real marriage, whether blended or traditional, takes work and sacrifice. So let's let first things be first. My grandmother used to say "you take you with you wherever you go." The truth of the matter is the only thing anyone can truly control is their own self. So, before you say 'I do', take a good honest look at yourself. What is your background? How were you raised? What are your expectations for marriage? What do you like? What do you dislike? What is your vision for life? What is your call? What are your strengths? What are your weaknesses? What will you put up with?

After you ask yourself all of the questions that you can possibly come up with, you then must ask the same of your future spouse. You're looking for things that won't quite mesh after your dating stage giddiness wears off. For instance, if you're both strong personalities and have a need to be in charge, will one of you be willing to back down if there is an impasse?

If you're entering into a blended family, it is imperative that you discuss your thoughts about child-rearing, discipline, and authority in the home. If children will be living in your home and there is any possibility at all, you should have a conversation with your former spouse or the non-custodial parent about your parenting style and your expectations for your household.

If you talk long enough and honestly enough, you may run across what I call are 'deal breakers'. Deal breakers show up when your viewpoints are so opposing on an issue that it will eventually cause a severe breach in the relationship. It's better to walk away ahead of time, than to divorce later.

If you make the determination to move forward with marriage, your primary aim should be to focus on becoming the best 'you' that you can be. If you enter into a marriage with the mindset that you will change the other person, you will be sadly mistaken. People experience lasting change only when they truly want it and want to work for it.

If there are children involved, sufficient time should be given for the children to become acclimated to the new arrangements. You should talk to them honestly about what is going to happen. Explain things at their level and give them time to respond and adjust.

Ask God for the wisdom necessary to make the right choices before you say 'I Do.':

o   Be honest about some "crosses" that you expect to bear daily to make your blended family work. Talk about how you feel about the sacrifices you are making or will make. Discuss ways to make the other partner's "load" a little lighter.

o   Be honest and specific about areas you have identified where there is little or no agreement between you. Know ahead of time what your strong and weak points are as a couple, so that you'll have a defense against opposition.

o   Discuss in detail what circumstances will be unique to your new family. You take you with you wherever you go, so be honest about how you contributed to the breakdown of your former relationship(s).

o   Be honest about your expectations. Don't just go along with what you don't really agree with because it will become an issue later on.

o   Hash out EVERYTHING you want, expect, and will or won't do.

Let's Pray...

Father, you said in all of our getting to get understanding. I need your wisdom to make the right decision before saying 'I Do." Give me revelation knowledge and understanding into the true nature of everything that will affect me in this relationship. Give me the strength to walk away if it is not a good fit. Thank you for loving me enough to reveal truth. Amen.

Things to ponder:

1. Did you and your spouse discussed finances, discipline, and authority in your household? If so, did you reach consensus?

2. Set a date and determine to hash out everything you want, expect, and will or won't do. Don't hold back and take as much time as necessary to thoroughly discuss each issue.

3. If you're already married, how can this chapter benefit you?

NOTES:

_____
_____
_____
_____
_____
_____
_____
_____
_____
_____
_____
_____
_____
_____
_____
_____
_____
_____
_____
_____
_____
_____
_____
_____
_____
_____
_____
_____
_____
_____

Gaining the Advantage

During the French Revolution and early stages of World War I, Napoleon I of France used two primary strategies for the approach to battle. His "Manoeuvre de Derrière" (*move onto the rear*) was intended to place the French Army across the enemy's lines of communication. This "indirect" approach into battle also allowed Napoleon to disrupt the linear formations used by the opposing armies. The second strategy used by Napoleon when confronted with two or more enemy armies was the use of the central positioning. This allowed Napoleon to drive a wedge to separate the enemy armies. He would then use part of his force to mask one army while the larger portion overwhelmed and defeated the second army quickly. The fundamental tactic for gaining ground in war was to outwit one's enemy by using the element of surprise. Surprise or the 'startle response' was used to interrupt an ongoing action and redirect the attention to a new, possibly more significant event.

"Many marriages would be better if the husband and the wife clearly understood that they are on the same side."

~ Zig Ziglar

Notice how Napoleon's two main war strategies focused on blurring communications and causing separation. As believers, the bible tells us we have an enemy; his name is Satan. In John 10:10, the bible calls him the thief. His main purpose is to steal, to kill, and to destroy any and everything that represents God. I believe he is using the same tactics that Napoleon used, but he's using them against marriages today as he seeks to gain the upper hand. In fact II Corinthians 2:11 warns us not to be ignorant of this enemy's strategies or he will certainly get one over on us. It says, *"Lest Satan should get an advantage of us: for we are not ignorant of his devices."* The word 'advantage' in this passage actually means "to have the more, or to gain the greater share from another." The term 'devices' refers to the barrage of mental images, thoughts and perceptions that the enemy uses to flood our minds. His ultimate goal is to fulfill his evil purpose to destroy our family.

Whether this is your first or some subsequent other number of marriage, make no mistake about it you have an enemy that does not want this marriage to last. My grandmother used to give me this wisdom for enduring through difficult situations; she would say, "Start out so you can hold out." The idea being, that we should deliberately position ourselves so that we are not moved when under attack...no matter how bad things look.

In a blended family, the worst thing we can do is rely on our limited natural way of thinking or our past practices for handling marriage challenges. God knows us and he knows our spouse. He knows our failures and He knows our history, yet He still has a plan to give us the advantage. He has given us a tried and true strategy that will work for any situation, and all the while uncovering the enemy's plots and schemes against us. John 16:13 says Holy Spirit, the Spirit of Truth, *"He will lead us into all truth and will show us things to come."* God's strategy is to get wisdom FIRST and to let that wisdom guide our way. The only thing that can result when we operate in God's wisdom is that we win! In Proverbs 4:5-8, God says that wisdom will instruct us in every area of life. If we truly want to have success in marriage this time around, we're going to need the wisdom of God.

To have a good marriage will take God's wisdom, plus lots of work. You'll need to stay sharp. You choose – you can either work harder, or work smarter and wiser to gain the advantage to win over every challenge. Ecclesiastes 10:10 tells us if the axe is dull and never gets sharpened, then it'll take more effort to accomplish the task at hand. Operating in wisdom keeps the axe sharp, it always gives us the advantage, and it assures us success in the end.

The best offence is always a good defense. We know that the enemy hates anything and everything that God has created. Marriage and the family is the very first institution created by God. Consequently, the devil has launched a vicious onslaught against this institution that has been constant since the beginning of time. With this in mind, we must give ourselves and our marriages the advantage by seeking God's wisdom and staying on His plan. Here's some ways:

o Be willing to eliminate past practices and focus on a new way...God's way for handling difficulties. Make a commitment to get your wisdom from the Word of God first and stick to it!

o Learn to roll all the cares of your blended family over onto the Lord. He understands and knows the hurts you've encountered either from the past, or in your current marriage. We simply must learn to obey God's instruction and then trust Him completely.

o Pick your battles wisely. We become sharper through the fires of adversity. Focus on what is truly important. Recognize when the adversary is trying to throw up a smoke screen so he can divide and conquer. Decide not to fall for the same tactics over and over again. The more you overcome, the sharper you become. Remember, we win!

Let's Pray...

Father, you warned us not to be ignorant of the enemy's devices. I know that my spouse is not the enemy. Give us the wisdom that only comes from you so that we can win in our marriage today. Cause our communication to be clear and our thoughts to be pure so that we can maintain the victory that has already been won for us through Jesus Christ. Amen.

Things to ponder:

1. In what ways has Satan gained the advantage against you?

2. What principle from this chapter can you implement regain the advantage and close the door to the enemy?

3. Write out some goals and action steps to ensure the door stays closed to satanic influence.

   a.

   b.

   c.

   d.

NOTES:

_____

_____

_____

_____

_____

_____

_____

_____

_____

_____

_____

_____

_____

_____

_____

_____

_____

_____

_____

_____

_____

_____

_____

_____

_____

_____

_____

_____

_____

_____

Kids Do Matter

For children, divorce can be stressful, sad, and confusing. At any age, kids may feel uncertain or angry at the very prospect of mom and dad splitting up. As a parent, it's normal to feel uncertain about how to give your children the right support through your divorce or separation. It may be uncharted territory, but you *can* successfully navigate this unsettling time and help your kids emerge from it feeling loved, confident, and strong. The key is being able to redirect your attention away from the mayhem of your divorce or separation, and instead focus on confidently rearing our children according to God's Word."

Children are not merely our "possessions" but instead are the Lord's gift to us. When we became parents, our primary function became to exercise faithful stewardship for their lives." Yet, in the wake of death, divorce or separation, the state of the children's emotional health is usually the last thing that is considered. Studies have shown that the children are the ones most negatively impacted by the devastation of divorce, even

"Let no Christian parents fall into the delusion that Sunday School is intended to ease them of their personal duties. The first and most natural condition of things is for Christian parents to train up their own children in the nurture and admonition of the Lord."

~ Charles Haddon Spurgeon

if it doesn't seem so on the surface. They are the ones who are the least emotionally equipped and least mentally prepared to successfully navigate this unfortunate turn of events. They will often experience feelings of abandonment, guilt, anger, frustration, and feel forced to choose loyalties toward one parent or the other. As parents and guides in the home, put yourself in the child's shoes and try to see what they see and feel what they feel.

Since the children usually don't have much of a choice or a say so when it comes to their future because of their parent's decision to separate, it is crucial that the parents be mindful of the tremendous upheaval that occurs in a child's life when divorce or separation occurs. And, it doesn't really matter what ages the children are. If the loss is from divorce or separation, rather than the death of a parent, there have probably been many years of dysfunction in the home leading up to the divorce. If the children's emotional well-being is not handled properly, lasting damage can be inflicted unnecessarily.

First and foremost the kids need to know that what happened between you and their other parent was not their fault. They need to know that you genuinely care about how they feel and that you will try to understand their pain and loss. They need an opportunity to vent without reprisal, even if you don't like what they are saying or how they're saying it. It's also important for them to get their issues on the table so that you can help them know how to handle their feelings. Hebrews 4:14-15 shows us the Father's 'open-door' policy toward us. No matter what we've been through or how we've failed, we can come boldly and ask for grace and find the mercy we need to deal with our situation. We should afford that opportunity to our children as well.

How you, as the adults, have handled your negative emotions has much to do with what kind of atmosphere was established in your home. It is unrealistic to expect that the children will be able to control their emotions, when it has not been modeled in front of them. If you give them the space and guidance to work through whatever their feelings are, you will reap a bountiful harvest in the end. Proverb 103:8-14 provides a great model of how the Father deals with us and our shortcomings. He is merciful and gracious toward us. He hasn't dealt with us based on our shortcomings or our emotions. He is patient and understanding with us, while gently guiding our hearts to the right place. Allow your children the same grace that you expect to receive.

o   Tell your children the age-appropriate truth about what is happening. Communicate with them will enough to make them feel secure, protected and wanted.

o   Pay attention to any negative behaviors that may have arisen in your children since your divorce, or since you've remarried. Be the high priest in your home and seek to facilitate healing.

o   Gently guide your children through the process of dealing with negative emotions associated with your divorce or remarriage. Set the ground rules for respectful dialogue and then let them get everything out. Rather than judging or disciplining, attempt to see the situation from their perspective.

o   Work at making sure that your method of dealing with anger, frustration, rejection or guilt is in line with how the Bible tells us to respond. Attempt to be a Godly example of how to take what the enemy meant for evil can be turned to.

Let's Pray…

Father, our children didn't create this situation, we did. Give us the wisdom to care for and guide our children so that they come through unscathed. Speak to our hearts and tell us how to minister to each child in a way that pleases you and causes them to fulfill the plan purpose you have for their lives. Amen.

Things to ponder:

1. Have you noticed any negative affects in your children resulting from your divorce or separation?

2. What opportunities will you create for your children to be able to 'vent' their fears and/or frustrations in a healthy way?

3. Are you open to seeking out professional counseling if necessary for the benefit of your children? If not, why?

Cathy L. Wray

NOTES:

_____
_____
_____
_____
_____
_____
_____
_____
_____
_____
_____
_____
_____
_____
_____
_____
_____
_____
_____
_____
_____
_____
_____
_____
_____
_____
_____
_____

A Matter of Discipline

One of my colleagues wrote this statement for *Today's Modern Family* a few years ago, "Blending a family isn't easy and it can present a unique set of challenges where discipline is concerned. Co-parenting requires not only cooperation between the responsible parents, but it also requires consistent discipline. Oftentimes even biological parents will have differing views when it comes to disciplining their child. But, these differences are usually magnified times 10 within the blended family unit. They can sometimes destroy a marriage, if they aren't properly dealt with from the beginning."

"A child who is allowed to be disrespectful to his parents will not have true respect for anyone."

~Billy Graham

As we've already discussed in previous chapters, children who are products of divorce and separation often experience a tremendous amount of unrest in the wake of their parents break-up. This makes tackling the issue of child discipline much more complicated, but necessary nonetheless. In order for the blended family to truly be successful in this area, matters of discipline must be well thought out, firmly substantiated in God's Word, and administered with love and compassion.

How and when discipline will be administered should be a thoroughly discussed, well thought out plan that ALL of the parents (if possible) have discussed and agreed to well before it is needed. Depending on the ages of the children, any physical correction may need to be meted out in progressive stages as it relates to the non-biological parent in the home, and should only come into play after the non-biological parent has established a 'love presence' first. A love presence happens when the non-biological parent takes the time and measures necessary to form a loving bond and establish trust with the children. This assures the children and the biological parent that the non-biological parent truly cares for the well-being of the child and is not just acting out their aggressions or frustrations.

One major mistake parents often make is overcompensating for the breakdown of a previous marriage by not establishing any plan for discipline at all. This is a recipe for disaster. Proverbs 22:15 tells us that all children need to be trained, corrected, and disciplined at some point. If this correction doesn't happen, the end result will bring the entire family to shame. And, certainly don't make the mistake of expecting your spouse (who may be the non-biological parent) to contribute to the home financially, emotionally and otherwise, but then allow them no voice and no position of authority over your biological children.

As much as is humanly possible, try to include the biological parent not living in the home into the plans for disciplining the children. This will help eliminate misunderstandings in the future and allow the children to see that all of the parents are on the same team as it relates to their upbringing.

Lastly and most importantly, always, always, always present a united front. If you must disagree (and there will be those times), do it in private. The nature of children can sometimes be manipulative and they will play one parent against another to save their own behind. Once you make a decision, stick with it and then back each other up. If there is an impasse, take a break, pray it out, talk about it, and don't do anything until you agree.

o   Discuss a logical progression for integrating the non-biological parent into a disciplinarian role. Finds ways to facilitate the proper level of respect, whatever your form of discipline. Never allow the children to cause you and your spouse to side against one another. If you disagree on a matter of discipline, talk about it in private and present the final edict as one unit.

o   No discipline at all, or lop-sided discipline will eventually sabotage your family structure and work against what you're trying to accomplish as parents. Make sure that both parents in the home (biological and non) are recognized as authorities and expected to be obeyed.

o   Get all the cards on the table...discuss ways to include your child's other parent in the plans. He/she is still a parent and has a right to know what is going on with their child. Be clear about how your house will be run. Talk about why this is important and be honest about challenges that your family my face when trying to carry out the plan.

Let's Pray...

Father, Thank you for the wisdom and the strength to raise our children in the way that you have shown us in your Word. Give us revelation knowledge and insight on how to set guidelines and give correction to our children. Help us to administer discipline out of love rather than anger, trusting that your Spirit will bring conviction and direction to our children as a result. Amen

Things to ponder:

1. What is the plan for discipline in your home?

2. Has it been a challenge incorporating your spouse's participation in the discipline of the children?

3. Has this chapter helped you understand the necessity for discipline in the home? If so, in what way?

NOTES:

_____
_____
_____
_____
_____
_____
_____
_____
_____
_____
_____
_____
_____
_____
_____
_____
_____
_____
_____
_____
_____
_____
_____
_____
_____
_____
_____
_____

Fight the Good Fight - Successful Conflict Resolution

"Fight the good fight of faith, lay hold on eternal life, whereunto thou art also called, and hast professed a good profession before many witnesses."
~I Timothy 6:12

Faith is literally defined as complete belief and trust in God that He will watch over His word, to have His word perform that which He has sent it out to do. Faith knows that the word of God will not return to Him void, and solid faith believes and trusts this. While the above statements are probably easier to hear than they are to actually do, God still expects us, as His children, to stand in faith, trust, and believe until the end. As for the fight itself - the good fight of faith; it is to believe that the Word of God works even when we can't see it working.

In context, I Timothy 6:12 is telling us to keep the faith through the hardships we may face so that we may have a good testimony before people who are watching us. Given the unique nature of the blended

"When you resort to shouting in conflict, you are reacting in the flesh. You have lost control of the only person you can control: yourself."

~Neil T. Anderson

36

family, there will be many, many opportunities to fight...the fight of faith that is. There is potential for misunderstandings ranging from baby mama drama to how, when, and who will administer discipline. The key to successful blended family life is in perfecting the art of conflict resolution.

It's more than naïve to think that you will live with any person long-term and never have differences of opinion. And, unless you truly are a door mat, there will come a time when you feel very strongly about an issue and will express your point of view accordingly. Let's keep it real! Ephesians 4:26-27 tells us in no uncertain terms that everyone will experience anger at some time or another. But it also gives us a strategy for handling that emotion so that it doesn't become something more than what we really intended or desired. It is important to be able to say what's bothering you, but there is always an appropriate way to get your topics on the table. From a spiritual aspect, anger negatively affects our spiritual sensitivity and receptiveness to God the Father and keeps us from operating in love and forbearance like the Word requires us to. Unchecked anger and unwillingness to reconcile can become a seething, brooding bitterness that will facilitate irreparable harm. These are dangerous emotions that always threaten to blow out of control. Lingering anger can easily turn into violence, emotional scarring, increased mental stress, and have many other destructive results. The good fight of faith is to believe and stand our ground using the Word of God against all odds, no matter how dark or hopeless the situations or circumstances may seem.

When we hang onto conflict, there is an open door for the enemy to bring division. The power of agreement is destroyed and our prayers become ineffective. How can two continue to walk together accept they agree? If you're in this marriage for the long haul and you want to experience it like God has designed, then you'll need to consider how to effectively handle conflict when it arises. Here are some helpful tips:

o   Maintain self-control. Remember the age-old rules of engagement for 'intense fellowship': a) Breathe, b) Wait until you calm down, and c) Seek to understand the other point of view. Do all this before you open your mouth!

o   Attack the issue not your spouse. Maintain self-control (no name calling and certainly no hitting, pushing, or shoving). If the situation is beginning to escalate, take a break and repeat the first set of Successful Resolution points.

o   Don't bring up past issues that are not relevant to the current problem.

o   Focus on solutions to the problem rather than the problem itself, b) Agree to disagree, then c) Forgive and let it go.

Let's Pray...

Father, your word tells us to pursue peace and to live peaceably with everyone if it is possible. Help us to pursue peace in our marriage. Teach us to fight the good fight of faith even when we disagree. Mostly, help us to make our marriage a testimony to those who may be watching us. Amen.

Things to ponder:

1. Have you been successful in resolving conflict in your marriage? If so, why do you think so?

2. List some of the challenges you face when attempting to resolve conflict:

    a.

    b.

    c.

    d.

    e.

    f.

    g.

3. What steps can you take personally to improve your conflict resolution skills?

NOTES:

Check Your Vital Signs

Whenever we go to see a doctor, the first thing that happens when you're called into the examination room, is a nurse or attendant begins to check your vital signs -- weight, blood pressure, heart rate, etc. Vital signs are measures of various physiological statistics that are necessary for a health professional to assess the most basic body functions. Vital signs are an essential part of a case presentation. They give the doctor a surface indication of how your body is functioning and if it's doing what it is supposed to.

Everything that is alive has vital signs that are a direct reflection of its health; including marriage and the family. In the medical field, there are four vital signs that are the standard for measuring health: temperature, pulse, pressure, and respiratory rate.

Temperature – Temperature recording gives an indication of the core body temperature. The main reason for checking body temperature is to detect any signs of infection or fever. Pressure checks ensure that there is adequate blood flow throughout the body and can

"My wife's actions are a mirror. The way that my wife is acting toward me says more about me than it does about her. It says something about her too, but if I can focus on my half of the equation, I'll make way more progress in resolving conflict and building a healthy relationship."

~Darrel Tiny

also be used to evaluate blockages. Pulse shows the physical expansion (or lack thereof) of the arteries. The respiratory rate gives an indicator of potential respiratory dysfunction and potential lack of oxygen getting into the blood and flowing to the brain.

Maybe you have found, like most married couples have, that the vital signs of your marriage are okay in some areas, but you see definite warning signs in others. There are ways to improve your marriage vital signs and prevent dis-ease and dis-function from entering in and harming your marriage and blended family.

Genesis 2:24 and Ecclesiastes 4:9-12 provide an outline that sets the stage for basic marriage health: 1) Leave, 2) Cleave, 3) Help/Aid, and 4) Protect. We can see clearly from these scriptures that God intended that the man along with his wife govern their family according to the Word of God. So, the composition of the home should never determine the structure or operation of the home. The structure of the household should be based on God's Word. The husband should be the head; the one who gives direction and vision. He should leave away from the influence of his parents, friends, etc. and receive his instructions directly from God. The wife should be submitted to that vision and assist in carrying it out. The husband and the wife should create an impenetrable bond; they should use all of their individual resources, gifts and talents to help one another succeed and together fulfill God's purpose. The children should be trained to respect and obey the authorities in the home. Whether your family is blended or not, children can be rather selfish-natured; they will have a tendency to try to play one parent against the other. If the husband and wife have not agreed to present a united front, you can count on disaster…especially in the blended family. You may not always agree on a particular issue, but always let everybody else think that you do. Handle your disagreements in private. When you come out, come out as ONE! When the husband and wife present a united front, the children, the exes, and the in-laws will eventually get the message about how your household runs. If there are any cracks in the family foundation, the enemy will find them and use them against you.

Outside influences should not dictate how your home functions. Be clear and concise about what is expected and what will and will not be allowed in your home. Communicate your expectations to your children that reside in the home long-term and on a visitation schedule. Communicate your expectations to ex-spouses and in-laws and be firm about how your household will run. Everyone else may not agree with you; and they don't have to, but you only are responsible for your household.

Here are 7 keys for keeping your marriage healthy and alive:

o   Be in agreement
o   Pray for one another daily
o   Deal with conflict privately, as soon as possible
o   Learn to forgive from the heart
o   Build genuine intimacy: emotional, physical, spiritual
o   Keep the fire burning in the marriage
o   Never again entertain the thought of divorce

Let's Pray...

Father, you said in your Word that you wanted above everything that we would prosper and be in health. But, we recognize that this promise is dependent on how our soul prospers. We pray today for health and prosperity in our marriage. We ask you to grow us up and grow us together so that our vital signs are strong and vibrant. Help us to block out outside influences, adhere to one another, help one another, and protect one another. Amen.

Things to ponder:

1. Have you allowed outside influences to dictate how your home functions? If so, who/what are the specific influences?

2. Can you identify any ways you can improve based on what you've read? If so, choose 3 of the 7 Keys for Keeping your Marriage Healthy and develop an action plan to make the necessary improvements

NOTES:

The Trust Factor

I once read that people believe
what you do more than what you
say and I've come to know that the
statement is true. Sometimes we
enter into relationships thinking
that the other party should simply
accept who we are and what we say
just because we put it out there. Not
so Amigo! Trust is one of those key
elements to a lasting relationship
that must be earned and continually
cultivated.

    In a blended family there are
several layers of trust that must be
developed...the new marriage, the
relationship with any children,
relationships with in-laws (new
and old), relationship with
extended families (new and old),
and relationships with ex-spouses.
When you got married, I know you
thought that it was just going to be
'me and you' against the world, but
the truth is you will most likely have
to deal extensively with all of the
relational groups identified above for
some time to come; not to mention
when the kids grow up, get married,
have kids, and on and on...

> "A marriage without
> trust is like a car
> without gas. You
> can sit in it as long
> as you want, but it
> won't go anywhere."
>
> ~Anonymous

46

My daughter recently posted a comment on a Facebook site about dads. In the post she described her dad (technically her non-biological dad) as someone who was always there and never made her feel anything but loved. She went on to say that when she settled on a husband, he would have to possess the integrity, consistency and care that her dad possesses. She was able to come to that conclusion because she had developed tremendous trust in her dad's character. Even though he was the non-biological father, he conducted himself in a way that demonstrated that he could be trusted and therefore loved.

When you put your word out there do you do what you have said? If you're in a blended family today, there is a reason for it...somebody didn't keep their word before, didn't keep their commitment, and/or didn't fulfill their promise. When it's the second time around (or third, or fourth...), subconsciously everybody is anticipating the next let down. Proverbs 20:6 says, in a nutshell, that every person will want to make everyone else think they're great, but are you more than just talk...you are your actions. Can your spouse and your children safely trust that you have their best interest at heart? When trust is one of the basic foundations of the blended family, all of the parts that were once makeshift will eventually become seamless.

Not always, but for the most part men can have issues with admitting they are wrong. They can know it but they won't always do something to correct what they have done wrong. No matter who you are, it is important to make an attempt to fix what you mess up. If you said something, did something, or misjudged a situation...say so and do what you can to make the other parties feel secure that you wouldn't deliberately do it again. When you cannot fulfill your promise are you big enough to acknowledge your wrong? If you spoke too harshly or made a judgment before you knew all the details, go back and apologize and find out what will make it right. This is especially important when you are trying to blend with non-biological children that are now a part of your family.

Webster's dictionary defines 'trust' as reliance on the character, ability, strength, or truth of someone or something. Make a commitment today to be someone who exhibits these qualities for your new family:

o **Do what you say**. Possibly the most important step to building a foundation of trust is to do what you say you will do.
o **Never lie**. Tell the truth even when the truth isn't going to make things pretty. If you never lie, your family will know that they can trust you.
o **Become a good listener**. When your spouse or your children feel they cannot express their true feelings, this leads to a break-down in trust.
o **Resolve outstanding issues quickly**. Don't allow resentments to grow and fester. When resentment sets in, trust is lost.

Let's Pray...

Father, Help me to become a person that can be trusted by my spouse and my children. Help me to be diligent and consistent so that they see the character of God through me. Help me to eliminate negative patterns that I've developed from my past so that I can be the best for my family now. Amen.

Things to ponder:

1. What are the layers of trust that must be developed and what steps have you taken to ensure that those layers are in place?

2. Has anyone ever let you down? If so, how did you feel?

3. What valuable principle did you learn from this chapter? How will you apply it to your blended family?

NOTES:

The Art of Raising Another Man's Child

Fathers can become fathers at times by accident, but this is never true of a non-biological (sometimes referred to as 'step') father. Each non-biological father has made the deliberate choice to not only be a father, but to accept a role vacated – for whatever reason – by someone else.

While researching this topic, I ran across this statement from a boy named Joshua:

"Children do not get the luxury of picking their parents; nor are parents afforded the opportunity to pick their children...except of course, for stepdads. You chose to have me in your life, and while not every day will you be greeted with a time formally set aside to thank you, it is never far from my mind. Thank you for choosing to be such an important part of my life, for putting up with me even though you never had to, and for teaching me all that I would ever need to know about what it takes to be a real father."

Joshua obviously realized that it takes a certain quality of man to

"It takes a strong man to accept somebody else's children and step up to a plate another man left on the table..."

~ Ray Johnson

51

raise another man's children. A man who steps into this role cannot be insecure or overly sensitive. It's not a job for the faint-hearted; you must truly know who you are in Christ. If you are a man, raising someone else's children, here are some challenges you can expect to face:

o Rejection
o Rebellion
o Disrespect
o Blame
o Isolation
o Anger
o Hatred
o Division
o External Influences
o Low Self-Esteem
o Under-Appreciation
o Personal Attack
o Being Taken for Granted
o Sabotage
o Being Misunderstood

Don't despair! God has fully equipped you for the task at hand. I think Joseph was one of the best examples of how to be a father to those you haven't physically fathered. Joseph and Mary lived in a time when family and personal reputation were extremely important. Mary is pregnant with Jesus before she and Joseph are officially married, and the baby is not Joseph's. The angel of the Lord came to convince both Mary and Joseph that this was an act of God, but I'm certain all of the family and friends were probably not so persuaded. In Matthew 1:20, the angel of the Lord appeared to Joseph in a dream to bring comfort to him for what was about to happen. *"...Fear not for to take unto thee Mary thy wife: for that which is conceived in her is of the Holy Ghost.*" The word 'fear' in this scripture, is the Greek word *phobeo*. It's where we get our English word phobia. The angel was actually admonishing Joseph, "I know this child is not biologically yours, but don't be afraid to marry this woman and lead this family." Men, there is a certain empowerment that comes with the assignment of leading a blended family. If you're willing to see the big picture and recognize the fact that God is personally using you to help your non-biological child(ren) reach their God-given destiny, there will be tremendous rewards for both you and them in the end.

The children in your blended family have already gone through a lot. God can use you to provide the structure, affirmation, consistency, acceptance, and Godly example that they will need to see.

As Joseph raised Jesus, he faced all of the challenges that are present today when raising a blended family. There was probably gossip and rumors from the neighbors about how Joseph wasn't Jesus' 'real' dad. There were, more than likely, opinions from well-meaning relatives and in-laws. And, what about when Jesus' other sisters and brothers came on the scene? I'm sure they could calculate...they eventually realized that Jesus had a different dad. I can imagine there were conversations about preferential treatment, household chores, family inheritance, and so on. But, scripture never gives any indication that Joseph relinquished or shied back from his responsibility to lead, nurture, and groom ALL of his children for their destiny.

Regardless of the complexities that may come with the blended family, when the man of the home steps up to the plate and becomes the father and husband that God has designed him to be, order will begin to form and destinies will begin to take shape. Here are some tips that may make your job a little easier:

Know that your assignment is from God. Keep your eyes on Him and follow His design.

- o Be patient. Adjustment and change take time.
- o Don't take things personal. There will be times of resistance, rebellion, and down-right defiance. This too shall pass.
- o Each stage of child's development has its own inherent challenges for a parenting. Recognizing what those stages and challenges are will better assist you in dealing with your non-bio child's response and or reaction towards you.
- o Pray, Pray, Pray!

Let's Pray...

Father, Thank you for trusting me enough to use me to help mold someone else's future. Help me to be able to see the big picture for the task ahead of me. And, help me to continue to rely on your direction. Give me the wisdom I need to guide my family and minister to the needs of ALL my household. Amen.

Things to ponder:

1. What are some of the challenges you've faced while raising another man's child? Were you satisfied with how you handled them?

2. Prior to reading this chapter, how did you view your role/ assignment as it pertains to your non-biological children?

3. What is one valuable principle you learned from this chapter and how will you apply it to your blended family?

NOTES:

_____

_____

_____

_____

_____

_____

_____

_____

_____

_____

_____

_____

_____

_____

_____

_____

_____

_____

_____

_____

_____

_____

_____

_____

_____

_____

_____

_____

_____

_____

_____

Mission IS Possible

Sometimes, the hardest thing about being a blended family is the process of blending. I remember back a few years when I was attending leadership training for my job. The presenter had a number of things he was highlighting for the group: time management, dressing for success, oral presentation, etc. One of topics that really stood out to me was the one done on developing a mission statement. Developing mission statements is an exercise often done in corporate or business settings, but is very rarely something that is focused on in marriage.

Proverbs 29:18 says, "W*here there is no vision, the people perish…*" Another version says, "…*the people cast off restraint.*" In other words, when you have a mission, it subconsciously sets your mind on course for where you're headed and then programs your brain to cause you to accomplish it. Without a mission, we inadvertently tell our inner selves that we have no place to go and, that anything will suffice along the way.

"People get married without doing their homework. Too many people have the wrong mission. They are getting married at the infatuation level and when hard times come, it falls apart."

~Bridget Brennan

God has already established the framework for how the family is supposed to run. I Corinthians 11:3 says, *"But I would have you know, that the head of every man is Christ; and the head of the woman is the man; and the head of Christ is God."* If the foundation of the home is not properly laid then anything built on top of it will eventually collapse.

Husbands must lead, wives must support, and children must be taught to obey and to submit to authority. It is the father's responsibility to provide the vision and mission; giving the rest of the household something to line up with and hold on to. My husband has provided this kind of leadership for our family from the beginning. He has always cast vision, so we always had something to latch hold to as a family.

I was going through some old boxes and found our family mission statement that he put together from more than 20 years ago. I'll share it with you:

The Wray Family Mission Statement

Our objective: To collectively create a home atmosphere that promotes the spiritual, emotional, and physical well-being of each family member

We shall accomplish this by:

o   Providing unconditional love and acceptance for each family member.
o   Acknowledging each family member's individual uniqueness.
o   Praying for each family member on a regular basis.
o   Spending quality time together as a family doing activities that promote family unity.
o   Respecting each family member's personal privacy.

o Regularly encouraging and supporting family members in their school, work, sports, and in accomplishing their goals.

All of our five children are now grown and on their own. Some of them are even raising families of their own; but each of them are using their individual gifts and talents to reach the destiny that was in their hearts as young children.

Don't let another day get underway without taking time to find out what good things God has put in the hearts of each person in your family and creating an action plan to get each one of you to your appointed destination. Forget all of the disappointments, setbacks, and hardships from the past. Forge into the good and expected plan that God has planned for you. Why not establish a mission for your family...tell it where you want it to go...the Mission is Possible!

Let's Pray...

Father, Give us a visual of your plan for our lives. Help us to write the vision so that it will be plain and useful for guiding us into your purpose. Even though we've failed in the past, help us to forget the things of the past and reach forward to the place you have for us as a family. Amen.

Things to ponder:

1. In your own words describe the importance of a Family Mission Statement.

2. Gather your family members and use the space below to write out your own family mission statement:

NOTES:

_____

_____

_____

_____

_____

_____

_____

_____

_____

_____

_____

_____

_____

_____

_____

_____

_____

_____

_____

_____

_____

_____

_____

_____

_____

_____

_____

_____

_____

Establishing Realistic Expectations for the Blended Family

"A great marriage is not when the 'perfect couple' come together. It is when an imperfect couple learns to enjoy their differences." ~Dave Meurer

The number of women (and men) entering into marriage with unrealistic expectations is staggering. Very few of us have positive role models for a healthy, happy marriage. In the absence of healthy role models our ideas of what love and marriage should look like have been formed by Hollywood and Mills & Boons novels (Patel 2011).

"What had seemed easy in imagination was rather hard in reality."

~L.M. Montgomery

The unpopular truth is that marriage isn't glamorous. Marriage and married love isn't the sum total of one's sex life; marriage is about commitment. We didn't take the vows to love our spouse 'for better or worse' merely as something to do. As sure as night follows day, we will face problems, obstacles and challenges. You can decide to face the problems and challenges of life together or let them rip you apart. Marriage is about sacrifice, and anything that will ever become a success in life will require sacrifice.

Marriage is about tolerance and acceptance. Neither of you married a perfect person, so that means we must learn to accept and tolerate our spouse's faults, imperfections, and differences of opinions. I believe the scripture calls this forbearance.

Marriage is about compromise. Raquel Welch has this to say about compromise, "We all have a childhood dream that when there is love, everything goes like silk, but the reality is that marriage requires a lot of compromise." We live in a selfish generation, so compromise is not a hugely popular term. Compromise does not mean being subservient, it simply means that you are willing to meet your partner at the place where you can find a solution that both of you can live with when there is conflict.

Lastly, marriage is about giving. It's about being willing to meet your partner's needs with an attitude of love and a willing spirit. Many couples have the 50-50 mentality. Each partner feels that they will contribute 50% to the marriage and that the other partner must do the same, but life doesn't work that way and great marriages don't thrive in an atmosphere of score-keeping. Instead give it all you've got and put forth 100% effort into your marriage. Make the effort to be the best partner you can be, and 99 times out of a 100 your partner will return the favor.

You might be just starting this marriage, or several years into it. Whatever the case, it's never too late to begin to set realistic expectations for how you'll continue. Take some time to revisit where you are today and think about where you really want to be. And, remember:

o **Your spouse won't meet all of your needs.** Some people equate being in love and being married with your spouse meeting all of your needs all of the time. The truth is another human being will never be able to meet all of your needs. There is something on the inside of us that is designed so that only God can satisfy. Marriage does not negate your need for personal, intimate relationship with your creator.

o **A good marriage will require work.** People don't grow together by osmosis. If you don't devote the time, energy, and attention to your marriage, you will be divorced (whether legally or in your minds). A quality marriage requires that you spend time together; that you have a genuine interest in making one another happy, and that you're committed to stay committed through any hardships that may arise.

o **A good marriage is not 50/50.** 50/50 is what roommates do. Marriage is about supporting, praying for, and helping one another whether the efforts balance out or not.

o **You won't always 'feel' in love.** Sometimes people base their marital happiness on if they feel in love or not. If your marriage depends solely on how you feel, it won't survive. There will be times you feel in love, and times when you don't, but neither time should dictate the state of the marriage. Make a determination to just be married, whether you feel like it or not.

Let's Pray...

Father, Thank you for my spouse and thank you for our marriage. Forgive us for judging one another based on unrealistic and ungodly expectations. We no longer want to keep score, but we're willing to give our all to the success of this marriage. Helps us to see clearly, to work earnestly and pray fervently for one another. Amen.

Things to ponder:

1. Make a list of your expectations prior to marriage. Which ones would you deem as unrealistic today and why?

2. What are some realities you've experienced since you've been married? What adjustments, if any, have you made because of them?

3. List four of the "marriage is..." statements outlined in this chapter. How successful have you been in each of the areas you listed? (Be honest)

   a.

   b.

   c.

   d.

Cathy L. Wray

NOTES:

Leaders Lead...Period

In his book, *Soup*, Jon Gordon shares ten aspects of leadership that I think are phenomenal. I'll share just a few of them with you here:

1. People follow the leader first and the leader's vision second.
2. Trust is the force that connects people to the leader and his/her vision.
3. Leadership is not just about what you do but what you can inspire, encourage and empower others to do.
4. A leader brings out the best within others by sharing the best within themselves.
5. Just because you're driving the bus doesn't mean you have the right to run people over.
6. Lead with optimism, enthusiasm and positive energy, guard against pessimism and weed out negativity.

"A leader is one who influences a specific group of people to move in a God-given direction."

~ J. Robert Clinton

For any family, but especially for the blended family, having a solid family structure is critical to reaching family goals. In order for that to happen, everyone has to know, function in, and thrive in their respective roles. My husband always says, "Everything rises and falls on leadership." So it stands to reason that proper direction for the family will begin with proper leadership. The father/husband carries the primary burden for providing leadership in the family. The Greek word for father is the word *patar*. It means leader, nourisher, protector, and provider. In Genesis 2:15 when God created man, his first instructions to Adam were to provide leadership for the Garden of Eden. *"And the LORD God took the man, and put him into the Garden of Eden to dress it and to keep it."* In other words, Adam was to take responsibility and oversight for the entire garden.

Later in Genesis 18:19, I love how God describes Abraham, *"For I know him, that he will command his children and his household after him, and they shall keep the way of the LORD, to do justice and judgment; that the LORD may bring upon Abraham that which he hath spoken of him."* God could trust Abraham because He knew he would lead, and because he was a leader, his family would follow. I Timothy 5:8 says, *"But if any provide not for his own, and especially for those of his own house, he has denied the faith, and is worse than an infidel."* Notice that both these scriptures show that leadership and provision should cover your "own" **as well as** those in your household. The term *'provide'* here means to perceive before or foresee the needs of. The term *house* refers to anything or anyone belonging to the household, whether related by blood or not.

In life things can get difficult. It's not always easy to provide leadership when you're conflicted or disappointed. But, leaders always lead…period. In First Samuel 30:1, King David was faced with some devastating news about his family, his property, and that of the men that were following him. He became extremely discouraged but in the face of the discouragement, he still provided leadership. In the aftermath those same men who previously wanted to stone him, followed him into yet another battle instead.

In Second Chronicles chapter twenty, King Jehoshaphat was facing insurmountable odds against himself and the children of Israel. But, leaders always lead...period. He knew that only God could give him the victory against the great army he was facing. So, he led his army and the entire nation in consecration and prayer so that God would give him the direction necessary.

Leading and managing a blended family is not for the faint-hearted. You must know who you are in Christ and fully accept that God made you to be the leader of your family. You can be confident that when you follow God's plan, He's got your back! Husbands get in your place; be the Godly example in your home. Provide the leadership necessary for your family to come out on top. Use everything God has given you in order to provide your wife and your entire household with vision, direction, provision, and protection. Leaders lead...period!

o   Fathers see ahead and think about what is needed for the entire household. Fathers supply leadership. Fathers model stability. Fathers love and care for not just their blood-related children, but for any children under their care.

o   Fathers bear the brunt of the hardship for the family. It's not easy, but God has equipped you to carry the load and be an example for everyone else to follow. When you stay in your role you'll find, just like King David, that God will give you the strategy for your family to have victory in every situation! Your wife and your children will admire and respect you more for your leadership.

o   Fathers order their families after God. Your family doesn't necessarily need you; they need the God in you! Leaders are not afraid to say "I don't know the answer, but I know who does and we will trust Him."

Let's Pray…

Father, help me to provide loving protection for my family and guidance for my entire household. I pray that you will constantly inspire and motivate me to do and to be all that you have called me to. When I'm down or discouraged, build me up with your word so that I can continue to lead in every situation. Amen.

Things to ponder:

1. In your own words how would you define leadership?

2. How important is leadership to your blended family?

3. On a scale of 1-10 (being the lowest) how would you rate your leadership?

4. What steps can you take to improve your leadership skills?

Cathy L. Wray

NOTES:

_____
_____
_____
_____
_____
_____
_____
_____
_____
_____
_____
_____
_____
_____
_____
_____
_____
_____
_____
_____
_____
_____
_____
_____
_____
_____
_____
_____
_____

The Difference is You

Frank Sinatra once recorded a song entitled "What a Difference a Day Makes." The final verse of the song ends with "... *the difference is you.*" Often times in marriage it's much easier to focus on the faults and shortcomings of your spouse. Without giving it much thought at all I'm sure we can look back over the years and systematically point out numerous, specific occasions when our spouse did or said something that we felt they shouldn't have. The problem, however, is that when it comes to our own shortcomings, the recollection gets a bit clouded.

> *"Be the change you wish to see..."*
>
> **~Mahatma Gandhi**

A cousin of mine has a favorite saying, "*...just clean up your side of the street.*" You see, if each person would clean their side of the street, the whole street would always stay clean. Cleaning your side of the street means you must focus on you first. Matthew 7:3-5 says, "*And why do you look at the mote that is in your brother's eye, but do not consider the beam that is in your own eye? Or how will you say to your brother, let me pull out the mote out of your eye; and, do not see that a beam is in your own eye? ...first get the* *beam out of your own eye; and then you can see clearly to get the mote out of your brother's eye."* You are the one that makes the difference.

In his letter to the Philippians, the Apostle Paul said, *"... brethren, I count not myself to have apprehended: but this one thing I do, forgetting those things which are behind, and reaching forth unto those things which are before, I press toward the mark for the prize of the high calling of God in Christ Jesus"* – Philippians 3:13-14 (KJV). Unfortunately, many times married couples ponder the past with regrets – wondering what they could've, should've, or would've done differently, especially if they've recently endured seasons of great challenge. If we'll take Paul's advice, times of reflection can become excellent opportunities to set goals for a brighter future. We don't have to be doomed to continue the negative cycles of the past. Should've, could've, would've is gone. Learn from the things that didn't work back then, figure out what is good for now, and then throw your past failures into oblivion.

In his book, *Maximize the Moment*, Bishop T.D. Jakes said, *"Stop rehearsing the past and start writing the rest of your story."* The good news for married believers is that we can absolutely determine the difference each new day makes for us! If things have been bad, we can make them good. Even if they've been good already, we can make them better. Begin to align your words with the Word of God. Hebrews 11:3 tells us that is, *"through faith we understand that the worlds were framed by the word of God, so that things which are seen were not made of things which do appear."* Frame the future of your marriage by saying what God says about you, about your spouse, and about your final outcome.

Make a decision today to:

o   Clean up your side of the street.
o   Set your sights on a brighter future.
o   Eliminate negative cycles of the past.

o   Use your words to sow seeds of love and grace.

o   Start writing the rest of your marriage story.

Let's Pray...

Father, I make a commitment today to work on me. I choose to let go of the past and embrace the bright future you have for me and our marriage. With your help, I'm changing my words...I'm re-writing our story. Our marriage will thrive and succeed! Amen.

Things to ponder:

1. In your own words write out what Matthew 7:3–5 means to you.

2. Describe a time when you blamed your spouse for not being up to par, but it was you who dropped the ball.

3. How will you make the difference in your marriage and family?

NOTES:

_____

_____

_____

_____

_____

_____

_____

_____

_____

_____

_____

_____

_____

_____

_____

_____

_____

_____

_____

_____

_____

_____

_____

_____

_____

_____

_____

_____

_____

Freedom from Fear and Failure

Between 1929 and 1945, the American people experienced two periods of great devastation: the Great Depression and World War II. In his book, *Freedom from Fear*, David Kennedy describes how Americans endured, and eventually prevailed, in the face of those unprecedented calamities. People had a choice during those times; they could give up on life or they could look for glimmers of opportunity that the future would hold.

When people marry they often don't realize that they bring fears into the relationship. Whether it's a fear of rejection or failure, fear can keep us from intimacy and satisfaction in marriage. If you've previously been in a failed marriage, subliminally it's easier to believe that it's not likely that any relationship could ever last a lifetime. There's something about failure that the enemy uses to try to reprogram our thinking. You see, God intended that we always win and when our lives take us in a direction opposite from winning, we subconsciously begin to doubt that it's possible to absolutely win at

"Achievement seems to be connected with action. Successful men and women keep moving. They make mistakes, but they don't quit."

~Conrad Hilton

everything. The devil ultimately wants convince us that, not only did our marriage fail, but that we ourselves are failures. He desires us to stay in confinement and in bondage to our past scars. I've got a news flash for you...just because you've failed in a previous marriage, doesn't mean you're a failure and it doesn't have to be the final say for marriage or for you.

If you plan on moving forward in this marriage based on your past track record or your individual abilities, you probably are not capable of creating a successful marriage this time either. But, Christ died so that we could live in victory and freedom. He died to set us free from the bondage of this world and from the torment our past. II Timothy 1:7 tells us emphatically that *"God has not given us a spirit of fear, but one of power, love and of a sound mind."* No matter how you feel or what has happened in the past, you have the ability to be married successfully and to live in harmony this time around.

In the third chapter of Philippians, the Apostle Paul encourages believers to forget whatever was in the past; whatever things that happened that did not line up with God's plan and purpose for their life. In Philippians 3:13-15 Paul says, *"Brethren, I count not myself to have apprehended: but this one thing I do, forgetting those things which are behind, and reaching forth unto those things which are before, I press toward the mark for the prize of the high calling of God in Christ Jesus. Let us therefore, as many as be perfect, be thus minded: and if in anything ye be otherwise minded, God shall reveal even this unto you."*

This passage of scripture is really telling us how we can successfully move away from our old reality; even if it's a reality that we created. The word "forgetting" in Philippians 4:13, is translated as **epilanthanomai.** It means to cast over into oblivion. This word is presented in the active present tense, which means that we always have to be forgetting the things that are in the past. The word "reaching" in that same verse is also in active present tense. It comes from the Greek word **epekteinomai**. It means that we are always stretching forward toward something.

The Apostle Paul understood this concept better than most. The scriptures tell us that before his conversion on the road to Damascus, Paul was the main persecutor of the church. Acts 8:3 says, *"…Saul [Paul]…made havoc of the church, entering into every house and haling men and women committed them to prison."* But, if we read Second Corinthians 7:2, Paul says *"Receive us; we have wronged no man, we have corrupted no man, we have defrauded no man."* He got the revelation that past failures didn't have to dictate his future.

Whatever things have happened in the past, we can't change. My daughter would say, "It is what it is." Stop holding on to the hurts and memories of past relationships and give them to the one person who can truly carry all of your burdens. Today is the time to let go and give it to the Lord so that your marriage is a safe haven free from the fear of failure.

Here are some tips:

o   Be honest with yourself and your spouse about your fears.
o   Trust in the God of your future more than the experiences of the past.
o   Put your complete confidence in God's character and commitment to perform His word for you and your new family.
o   Don't look back…just keep moving forward.

Let's Pray…

Father, I realize that I've made mistakes in my past relationships. I receive your forgiveness for those mistakes and am determined to walk in your ability for my future. Thank you for the spirit of power that is working in me and helping me to make this marriage a success. Amen

Things to ponder:

1. What fears or apprehensions did you bring into the marriage?

2. In what way did your fears affect the quality of your relationship?

3. What steps are you willing to take to overcome your fears and create a successful marriage?

NOTES:

_____
_____
_____
_____
_____
_____
_____
_____
_____
_____
_____
_____
_____
_____
_____
_____
_____
_____
_____
_____
_____
_____
_____
_____
_____
_____
_____
_____
_____

Ending the Fatherless Generation

The Word of God tells us everything we need to know about living Godly and having success in every aspect of our lives. God is a God of covenant and when He made covenant with us, He promised that the blessing of that covenant would pass down to our children to as far as a thousand generations. With every covenant comes a commitment from all of the parties involved to fulfill their part. Well, God has done His part and if we read the scriptures in context, raising and teaching the children is our part as parents. More specifically, the impartation of Godly values was intended to be primarily the responsibility of the fathers.

I came across some alarming statistics on the internet the other day regarding the devastating effects of fathers being absent from the home:

o 63% of youth suicides are from fatherless.

"I cannot think of any need in childhood as strong as the need for a father's protection."

~ Sigmund Freud

o   90% of all homeless and runaway.
o   85% of all children who show behavioral.
o   80% of rapists with anger problems come from fatherless homes.
o   71% of all high school dropouts come from fatherless homes.
o   75% of all adolescent patients in chemical abuse centers come from fatherless homes.
o   70% of youth in state-operated institutions come from fatherless homes.
o   85% of youth in prison come from fatherless homes.

Researchers at Columbia University found that even children living in a two-parent household, but who had a poor relationship with their father were 68% more likely to smoke, drink, or use drugs compared to all other teens in two-parent homes. It seems that despite the popularity of the Women's Lib and Feminists movements, study after study has shown that no other factor is more vital to the healthy development of children than having a father in their life. This may be stretching it, but I believe the single greatest tragedy of our society today is the failure of fathers to take their responsibility as parents seriously.

God gave the responsibility of raising the children to the parents...specifically to the father. Throughout scripture, God speaks to fathers about how to teach, train, discipline, and model Godly principles to their children. But, for decades now we have witnessed the erosion of the traditional family along with the societal stability that mirrored that family unit.

I love God...no matter how the enemy slips in, He always has a solution to get us back to His original plan. This is true concerning His plan for the family as well; look at Deuteronomy 24:17-18 where the scripture says, *"Do not deprive the alien or the fatherless of justice...remember that you were slaves in Egypt and the Lord your God redeemed you from there. That is why I command you to do this."* God in all of His sovereignty knew what our modern-day plight would be. Just like in the days of old, He knew that He would need men – real men to step up to the plate and make a commitment to children who would otherwise be strangers and aliens. Today He is commanding men who will fill in the gaps, who will show up to basketball games, who will help with homework, and who be fathers to families for His glory.

Let's put an end to the fatherless generation:

o   If you're a father, make a new commitment to father your children wherever they are. Even if children don't reside in your home, it does not negate your God-given responsibility to them.
o   If you're a father to children that are not biologically yours, ask the Father for the wisdom to shape the children in your care for His divine destiny.
o   Be the Godly example in your home. Don't allow your wife or children to outdo your commitment to God.

Let's Pray...

God, help me to be a real father to my children. Give me understanding of your word so that I be a Godly example to my children and teach them how to live for you. Forgive me for not stepping up to the plate and cause me to be able to redeem the time that may have been lost. Amen

Things to ponder:

1. Did you grow up with your father in the home? What impact did his presence (or lack thereof) have on your life and development?

2. In what ways can you improve on your fathering skills?

3. If you're a mother, how will what you've read affect your choice in a future spouse?

NOTES:

_____

_____

_____

_____

_____

_____

_____

_____

_____

_____

_____

_____

_____

_____

_____

_____

_____

_____

_____

_____

_____

_____

_____

_____

_____

_____

_____

_____

_____

Build the Marriage, Save the Family: Establishing Genuine Intimacy

"Nothing can bring a real sense of security into the home except true love." ~Billy Graham

According to a study conducted by Wake Forest University on marriage satisfaction, a good marriage does more to promote life satisfaction than money, sex, or even children. Good marriages don't happen by accident, they are good because they are made that way on purpose. If we were to poll 100 couples on what makes for a good marriage, I'm sure we would come away with a myriad of answers. But, most couples would probably agree that open honest communication, genuine intimacy, and lots of sex are in the top three… with sex most likely as number one. The sex part shouldn't be surprising since sex in marriage is God's idea. It is His blessing to husbands and wives. It is His provision for making children, expressing intimacy, and providing pleasure to married couples whom He loves. Take a

"Sexual expression within a marriage is not an option or an extra. It is certainly not, as it has sometimes been considered, a necessary evil in which spiritual Christians engage only to procreate children. It is far more than a physical act. God created it to be the expression an experience of love on the deepest human level and to be a beautiful and powerful bond between husband and wife."

~John MacArthur

brief moment to thank God for sex! Now that we have the preliminaries out of the way, let's get down to the brass tacks... sex does not equal intimacy in marriage.

The latest Census Bureau data available for couples married between 1979 and 1988 showed that less than half of this group was still married at the 25 year mark. Only 58% of Americans were married to the same spouse after 25 years of marriage, and that percentage drops to 54% after 30 years of marriage.

I don't think people go through all the trouble of getting married just to get divorced or to waste a few years being single and then start over again with somebody brand new. People don't just fall out of love and marriages don't end overnight either... they die little by little. The death of a marriage begins to set in because people fail to recognize the enemies to the marriage. II Corinthians 2:11 tells us that if we are ignorant of the devices that Satan uses against us, then he will take advantage of us. This is certainly true in marriage. Ecclesiastes 1:9 says, *"...there is* no new *thing under the sun..."* Satan hasn't changed his game at all. He still uses his sly, subtle tactics to covertly draw us away from our marriage, and even more significantly, our marriage commitment. You see, oftentimes couples will remain in the institution of marriage without truly engaging in the true union of marriage. They've gone through the ceremony, they haven't filed for the divorce, yet they haven't become one.

Here are some of enemies to marriage:

o **Familiarity.** Don't make the mistake of letting things fall into a rut. Do your best to stay interested and to be interesting.

o **Apathy.** Apathy in marriage comes from two main sources: 1) the lack of motivation and excitement, and 2) the suppression of passion. Suppression of passion is usually the result of one party either, actually or in their perception, feeling like they have been victimized repeatedly. Lack of motivation and excitement comes after they've tried to address it and have been ignored. (All of this happens over time). A person who repeatedly communicates their frustration to the spouse, but never feel heard, they will give up hope. Conversely, the spouse who keeps trying to appease but whatever they do is "never good enough", they will give up hope.

o **Lack of Intimacy.** Whatever the reason behind divorces, couples from a long lasting marriage say that it is communication, and time spent together that make a marriage last long.

o **Taking each other for Granted.** Two main ways people take each other for granted are a) *Lack of acknowledgment and consideration for the other person:* Not thanking your partner when they do something nice for you; Not acknowledging your partner verbally or with eye contact when they are speaking; Not being considerate of your partner's time by being late; Not letting your partner know that you appreciate the small things they do each day; and b) *Using your partner to meet your needs:* Objectifying and pigeonholing your partner into specific roles and not seeing them beyond those roles; Expecting that your partner should meet all your sexual or other needs without giving anything in return; Expecting your partner to carry the financial responsibility for the household; Expecting your partner to look after all the household chores.

o **Sex.** Absence of sex in a marriage has a much more powerful negative impact on a marriage than good sex has a positive impact.

o **Creativity**. Try getting outside the box and doing some things that are out of your normal routine.

o **Invest in each other's Dreams.** Find out the hopes and aspirations of your spouse and actively look for ways to make their dreams come true.

o **Learn to forgive and let it go.** You can never move forward while looking backward. Decide today to let go of the past so that you're free to grab hold of your future.

Let's Pray...

Father, help me not to be afraid to let down the barriers that keep me from experiencing true intimacy in marriage. I choose to walk in your forgiveness daily for my shortcomings, and I refuse to hold ought against my spouse. Knit our hearts together so that we become a true representation of Christ's love and commitment to the Church. Amen.

Things to ponder:

1. What is your definition of intimacy compared to your spouse's?

2. How have your definitions of intimacy either unified or divided you?

3. Which enemies of marriage have you allowed to come into your marriage? How do you plan to rid your marriage of these enemies?

NOTES:

_____

_____

_____

_____

_____

_____

_____

_____

_____

_____

_____

_____

_____

_____

_____

_____

_____

_____

_____

_____

_____

_____

_____

_____

_____

_____

_____

_____

_____

_____

Avoiding the Fatal Five

Winston Churchill said "All men make mistakes, but only wise men learn from their mistakes." If you're in a blended family, you no doubt have already made your share of mistakes in marriage. The real problem with making mistakes is not in the making, but in the repeating. Marital mistakes that are left unresolved can result in the slow agonizing death of the marriage. For couples who have already fallen prey to some of the common mistakes, you can reverse the affects of those mistakes and begin to repair your marriage relationship today. I know it may seem easier said than done, but here are some definite traps to avoid:

1. **Disregarding Your Spouse's Opinion**

Disregarding your spouse's opinion is dangerous territory. It sends the message that, "My opinion is more valid than yours." It's okay to disagree but it's important to show that you can validate and attempt to understand your spouse's point of view even when you disagree.

"A man goes to knowledge as he goes to war, wide awake, with fear, with respect, and with absolute assurance. Going to knowledge or going to war in any other manner is a mistake, and whoever makes it will live to regret his steps."

~Carlos Castaneda

Unfortunately, sometimes one spouse regularly discounts the other's opinion. For example, a wife may assume she knows more about parenting and proper discipline than her husband. As a result, she may argue with him about his childrearing techniques because she assumes he's less educated about "the right way to do it."

Although there will always be some areas where one of you has more expertise than the other, it doesn't mean you can't still value one another's opinions. Don't treat your spouse like a child if you happen to know more about a certain subject. Learn to listen and develop an understanding of your spouse's point of view so you can make healthy decisions as a team.

2. Treating Others Better than Your Spouse

Most people are polite to co-workers, friends and extended family. Yet for some reason, can't find it in their psyche to offer their spouse simple common courtesies. The exact opposite should be true. A spouse should get your best moods, most of your attention, the bulk of your energy, and the rewards of your hard work.

When you're excited about something, the first phone call you should make should be to your spouse. Don't call a friend or your mother first to share the good news. Instead, make sure your spouse is the first one in line to hear about your promotion, a raise or just to hear about that funny thing that happened to you earlier in the day.

When you're in a bad mood, don't take it out on your spouse. Instead, work hard, just like you most likely would with a friend or co-worker, to show respect and kindness. Practice patience and use kind words, even when you don't feel like it.

3. Dishonesty

Dishonesty can be a slippery slope. Sometimes people start out lying about what they consider to be small things. For example, saying, "I only spent $100 today at the store," when you really spent $150 might seem like a small thing, but it is dishonest.

Sometimes people avoid telling the truth out of an effort to spare their partner's feelings, but learn to speak the truth in love. Your true feelings somehow have a way of coming out eventually.

Sometimes dishonesty is meant to avoid consequences. A wife might avoid telling her husband that she forgot to pay the phone bill on time and as a result, they have a late charge, because she knows her husband will be mad. She doesn't want to face his anger, so she tries to cover up the mistake by keeping their account information secret.

Over time, telling lies gets easier. If a person tends to lie about small things, it can become much easier to lie about the big things. It's important to be honest with your spouse at all times in order to build trust, work through issues and maintain a healthy marriage.

4. **Holding Onto Unrealistic Expectations**

Romance novels, TV shows, and movies tend to glamorize love and romance. It can lead to people holding onto unrealistic expectations about how marriage should be. This unrealistic expectation can lead to disappointment and always thinking the grass is greener on the other side.

Sometimes people look at other couples and think, "I wish we had that." It's important to remember that what you see on the outside isn't likely an accurate representation of what goes on behind closed doors. No marriage is always about romance and marital bliss.

It isn't realistic to expect that you'll always feel excitement when your spouse walks in the room or that your spouse will be able to meet all of your needs all the time. Instead, marriage is about working together as a team which means you won't always get what you want. And over time, those "in love" feelings shift to a more mature sort of love. It's natural.

Accepting that it's natural that you will fight sometimes and that you'll have to put a lot of effort into your relationship is important. It's also essential to develop realistic expectations of your spouse and your marriage as you navigate changes. Talk about what you expect from one another when you have children, change jobs or experience any changes in your marriage to ensure that you both have a clear understanding of what life will realistically be like.

5. **Allowing Resentment to Build**

Allowing resentment to build is not healthy for a marriage. It involves a feeling of bitterness that often stems from a feeling of betrayal in an intimate relationship. Resentment tends to get worse with time if it is not adequately dealt with.

It's your responsibility to make changes if you notice you are growing resentful. It's not your spouse's fault that you feel that way. Instead, take it as a sign that you need to do something different.

For example, a wife might grow resentful because her husband doesn't do enough chores around the house. She has several choices in how she responds to this. If she continues to do all the chores while growing bitter, it won't be healthy for their marriage. Instead, she can talk to her husband about her feelings, do fewer chores, or accept that a clean house just isn't as important to him. No matter what she decides to do, it's important that she take action instead of simply continuing to do the same thing while building resentment.

If you've already started to build some resentment, it's important to take action now. It won't go away on its own. Instead, there's work to be done that sometimes takes professional counseling to ensure that you can let go of bitterness and improve your marital satisfaction.

Mistakes made in your marriage don't have to be fatal - decide today to avoid the fatal five.

Let's Pray...

Father, Help us not to repeat the mistakes of the past, but rather move forward into your plan and purpose fo rour lives. Keep our hearts tender toward you, so that you can guide us into your truth about our marriage and away from destructive habits, associations, and influences. Amen.

Things to ponder:

1. Which of the fatal five have you violated?

2. What steps will you take to correct your actions?

NOTES:

_____

_____

_____

_____

_____

_____

_____

_____

_____

_____

_____

_____

_____

_____

_____

_____

_____

_____

_____

_____

_____

_____

_____

_____

_____

_____

_____

_____

Train up a Child

Even though my parents were not practicing Christians when I was growing up, they sent my sisters and me to church with any relative who would pick us up on Sundays. Most of my relatives embraced the Pentecostal doctrine, and as a result I had plenty of exposure to the 'charismatic experience' that included signs, wonders, miracles, and some other stuff too! Exposure has a tendency to create appetite; so I grew to anticipate seeing God move in some kind of way whenever we needed him and prayed earnestly for Him to show up.

Proverbs 22:6 says, *"Train up a child in the way he should go: and when he is old, he will not depart from it."* In this passage the word 'train' is the Hebrew word *chanak*. It references the palate and means to whet the appetite of a thing, or to create a bent toward something. This scripture is more about creating an appetite for the things of God in your children than it is about our specific parenting abilities. Our children could mean our congregations, those that we are discipling for Christ, or simply

"Exposure creates appetite, appetite ignites passion, passion causes action, and action produces results."

~Cathy L. Wray

those in our sphere of influence. As parents, our job is to give the exposure that creates the appetite! We do this by first being the example of what we expect our children to become. Let's face it, preaching sometimes has to be done without using words. Secondly, we must purposely place our children in situations and environments that allow them to taste the benefits of living and conducting themselves in a particular manner in order to produce desired results. Whether the children in your home are biological or non-biological, the desired end result should be the same. Because you physically bring a child into the world does not make you a parent. Parents are made because they do what is necessary to make sure their children have appetite.

I read the story of how former NBA star Shaquille O'Neal was raised, and it pretty much mirrors the point I'm trying to make. As a young teen Shaquille, who was being raised on a military base in West Germany by his biological mother and non-biological father, began to act out in school, get into fights, and sometimes had his skirmishes with the law. He did all this in hopes of being sent back to the U.S. to live with his biological father who had never made contact with him. However, Philip Harrison (Shaquille's step-father) put an end to that dream by telling Shaquille, "Look, son, no matter what you do, I'm not letting them send you back. And if you don't listen to me I'm going to beat your butt. Every...single...day." He was creating an expectation in Shaquille, that If you don't follow the rules there are consequences. He was also demonstrating genuine love to him. It would have been really easy to just send him to the states and be rid of him. Instead his actions said, "no matter what your behavior, you're my son and I'm going to love you through it. My job is to help you become a productive adult."

Exposure to love, structure, and consistency was creating an appetite in Shaquille for a lifetime of success and an attitude of a winner. After his retirement from a very successful career in the NBA, Shaquille stated in an interview with Sports Illustrated magazine, this about his non-biological dad… "I am not a hero, my [step-] father is my hero."

You may be raising the next Shaquille O'Neal or someone greater. The permanence of your impact will be in direct proportion to the amount of exposure you have created in your home. Here's some ways you can do this:

o   Change how you see things in your home. Your spouse is not your step-spouse, so the children in the home are not 'step' either. How you see them is how you will treat them.

o   Be firm. The children have most likely experienced an upheaval of sorts. They may act out or demonstrate any combination of various negative behaviors. Just hold the line…this too shall pass. Love never fails.

o   Parents Have a United Front! Whether you're blended or traditional, kids will sometimes find a way to play one parent against the other in order to get what they want. Make pact to never let the kids see you disagree. That doesn't mean that you will always agree, it just means that you'll disagree in private. If the kids know that they cannot penetrate the parental wall, things will progress much more smoothly than you can imagine.

Let's Pray…

Father, I believe your word and I accept my responsibility as a parent in my home. Thank you for the wisdom to create an environment that sparks the right appetite, and the insight to raise these children so that they each fulfill their God-given purpose in life. Cause me to be steadfast in my commitment to them just as you have been in your commitment to me. Amen.

Things to ponder:

1. Exposure creates appetite…What do you want your children to have an appetite for?

2. What spiritual things are you exposing your children to?

3. What natural things are you exposing your children to?

4. What educational and cultural things your you exposing your children to?

NOTES:

House Rules: Establishing Fairness & Equity in the Home

There is an adage in the business world that says, "people are our most important asset." However, if you've ever worked in corporate America, you know there are very few organizations that actually function as if they believe those words. Sadly, there are even far fewer families that operate based on this standard.

In a blended family there can be many layers that make up the family unit which give plenty opportunity for bias, favoritism, and neglect. For there to be peace in the home, every family member must know, understand, and agree on the rules of engagement, along with the consequences for violating them. Unfortunately, many parents make the mistake of making up the rules as they go; it might depend on what sort of mood they are in or which parent is home at the moment. Creating clear and concise house rules is an important step in establishing effective discipline

"Live so that when your children think of fairness and integrity, they think of you."

~H. Jackson Brown, Jr.

strategies and laying the foundation for peace and harmony in the home. Household rules are normally associated with chores, but more importantly should set a standard for how your family will operate in general. You won't be able to cover every possible scenario that could arise, but you can set a basic set of behaviors that your home will abide by. The rules will define how you live together and how you will interact with one another. Once in practice the rules will make the home more enjoyable for everybody.

It has been my experience that children will interpret rules to their best advantage – it's just the nature of a child. So, writing out and thoroughly discussing rules along with related expectations is essential. To make rules even more effective they should include set chores for all and specifically spell out that the behaviors and rules are for all to follow. Allocation of chores set the example that everyone is responsible for contributing to the upkeep of the home…it's everybody's house, whether they are on a visitation schedule or they reside in the home daily. Establishing desired behaviors sets the minimum standard of acting towards others, in the home and elsewhere. It is essential for each family member to know what the rules are.

o   Establish house rules that respect age-appropriate development for each of the children in the household. Obviously, teenagers will require a different level of independence than a toddler would.

o   Clearly outline what negative consequences will be in store when rules are broken, and stick to it.

o   Model the desired behaviors in front of your family. It's no longer the age of do as I say, not as I do.

Let's Pray...

Father, guide us as we set rules and guidelines in our home. Help us to be fair and equitable in all of our dealings, and to value each family member who is a part of our household. Give us the insight to establish our family's foundation on your word and not deviate from your principles. Amen.

Things to ponder:

1. Have you taken the time to establish clear, concise house rules? If so, what has been the impact on your family as a result?

2. Describe how setting household guidelines will help the individual members of your family.

Cathy L. Wray

NOTES:

_____
_____
_____
_____
_____
_____
_____
_____
_____
_____
_____
_____
_____
_____
_____
_____
_____
_____
_____
_____
_____
_____
_____
_____
_____
_____

Another Divorce is not an Option

I learned to ride a motorcycle about three years ago. During the motorcycle safety course there was section that covered making proper turns. The emphasis of the section was on rider focus. The prevailing theme was that whatever the rider was focused on is where the bike would end up going.

When a cycler fails to navigate a turn properly, it's usually a result of not focusing far enough ahead of the turn. The rider has to focus on where he wants to go...not where he is and not where he's been. The same is true if you've had a failed marriage and now want to try again. If your focus is on everything that went wrong the first time, you are destined to head in that same direction yet again.

In the third chapter of Philippians, the Apostle Paul encourages believers to forget whatever was in the past; the things that have happened that did not line up with God's plan and purpose for their life. In Philippians 3:13-15 Paul says, *"Brethren, I count not myself to have apprehended: but this one thing I*

"Marriage is the hardest thing you will ever do. The secret is removing divorce as an option. Anybody who gives themselves that option will get a divorce."

~Will Smith

do, forgetting those things which are behind, and reaching forth unto those things which are before, I press toward the mark for the prize of the high calling of God in Christ Jesus. Let us therefore, as many as be perfect, be thus minded: and if in anything ye be otherwise minded, God shall reveal even this unto you."

This passage of scripture is really telling us how we can successfully move away from our old reality; even if it's a reality that we created. The word "forgetting" in Philippians 4:13, is translated as **epilanthanomai.** It means to cast over into oblivion. This word is presented in the active present tense, which means that we always have to be forgetting the things that are in the past. The word "reaching" in that same verse is also in active present tense. It comes from the Greek word **epekteinomai**. It means that we are always stretching forward toward something.

The Apostle Paul understood this concept better than most. The scriptures tell us that before his conversion on the road to Damascus, Paul was the main persecutor of the church. Acts 8:3 says, *"...Saul [Paul]...made havoc of the church, entering into every house and haling men and women committed them to prison."* But, if we read Second Corinthians 7:2, Paul says *"Receive us; we have wronged no man, we have corrupted no man, we have defrauded no man."*

Whatever things have happened, we can't change that. My daughter would say, "It is what it is." But God is telling us that what is, can become what was. We can put what was, out of our remembrance and our meditations just as if it never existed. At the same time we can stretch our focus, thoughts and meditations forward to something new.

It's interesting that Paul chose a word that means to "stretch" because it denotes that it will take effort on our part to keep moving forward. Every day we must decide to throw the past into oblivion and stretch our thoughts forward to what God has in store. Every day that you are in Christ you must decide to become a person without a past. Tell yourself emphatically, "Not another divorce!" I won't focus on the past, but rather on the future that God has for me.

- o Remember that forgetting is ongoing forgiveness.
- o Don't meditate on the past.
- o Forgive yourself of past mistakes, sins, and bad decisions.
- o Choose to keep stretching forward.

Let's Pray...

Father, thank you for forgiving me of all the mistakes of my past. I believe you have a great plan for my future and I know this marriage does not have to end in divorce. Give me the wisdom and insight that I need to keep stretching forward and to become the spouse you fashioned me to be. Amen.

Things to ponder:

1. In what ways have you allowed failures from the past to determine your focus?

2. What steps can you take to ensure that your past can no longer dictate your future?

NOTES:

Dollars and Sense: Merging Finances

"For which of you, intending to build a tower, sitteth not down first, and counteth the cost, whether he have sufficient to finish it?" – Luke 14:28

Despite the image that the Brady Bunch tried to depict, handling finances in a blended family can be tricky. Any time a family is blended together the potential exists for added conflict, and financial conflict is always the worst kind in any relationship. Money issues are one of the major stressors of marriage in general, and most people have some emotional connection to their money. In blended families there are even more complicated money issues to resolve, making the stresses around finances even greater.

Blended families face special financial challenges. People marrying for the second time have lived independently for a while, and may have incurred substantial financial loss after divorce, division of assets, and being a single parent. Both spouses will probably bring

"After you marry, every asset either of you acquires is jointly held. That's why you both need to be in sync on your long-term financial goals, from paying off the mortgage to putting away for retirement. Ideally, you should talk about all this before you wed. If you don't, you can end up deeply frustrated and financially spent".

~Suze Orman

financial resources to the relationship, but they also bring their fair share of expenses. Some couples opt to maintain two bank accounts and keep their money separate. Others open joint accounts. Either way could work fine, as long as you're open with your spouse about how you're are saving, spending, and investing. Decisions about money should always be made together. Personally, I don't agree with being separate in marriage, however some blended families choose to establish a joint household account and joint savings for their life together and keep other accounts separate.

When two families join forces, "there's a financial implication around every corner," says financial planner Tim Maurer, of the Financial Consulate, in Lutherville, Md. So, it's important to keep in mind that legal and financial advice can keep your finances as healthy as possible if you are separated or divorced, or are in the process of creating a blended family. Here are a few blended family financial tips from resources such as: www.NewsForParents.org, www.e-personalfinance.com, www.Kiplinger.com/blended-family-finances that I found useful regarding marriage and blended family:

o **Set a Budget.** Consider your priorities, collectively. Determine what percentage of each individual's income will go toward the things that are important to the household. This amount should be calculated only after a certain percentage is set aside for savings. Always consider household expenses top priority. Such important priorities will most likely include:

- Savings
- Mortgage
- Household expenses like utilities and groceries
- Auto insurance and maintenance
- Medical bills
- Educational costs (college savings, school tuition)

Make sure you allocate these expenses at a rate that is fair to your mate and yourself by taking each person's salary into account. Make sure to agree on an allowance for any children, or on how college-age children will handle any money given to them. Also be sure to take into account any child support (for children not living with you), or alimony payments that are ongoing. These issues can be a major source of stress if they are not freely discussed.

o **Fair Does Not Mean Equal.** Blended families face an inherent potential for conflict, mainly because each parent ultimately feels obligated to care for their own biological children. The best way to deal with money-induced jealousy between stepsiblings is to sit down and talk about money with your children. Be honest; if you don't have the money, tell them. Believe it or not, kids are fully capable of understanding financial friction within a family. Even traditional families have been known to give one child more financial support than another.

o **Plan for the Future.** Remember to update your estate plan when you remarry. This involves changing the beneficiary on your RRSPs, insurance, workplace pension, etc. You'll also want to update your will and your power of attorney in order to protect your assets and your children's inheritance. Traditionally, your assets flow to your spouse, with the intention that they will eventually be dispersed to your children. However, this isn't always the case in a second marriage. In a worst case scenario, your second spouse could decide to give all of your assets to his children, effectively ignoring your biological offspring. For this reason, you'll want to talk to a financial advisor to make sure that your estate is arranged in a way that properly allocates your funds according to your desires.

o **Grow Together.** Before you make any decisions, remember to discuss them with your new partner. At the end of the day, the most important thing is to ensure that your entire family's needs are met, and that financial issues aren't hindering your ability to grow together in a strong, unified and lovingly *blended* way.

Remember, rely on the wisdom from the Word of God for every decision you make. Before you make another move, spend time in prayer in the study of the Word. Then follow God's instructions as you establish the finances in your home.

Let's Pray...

Father, we surrender our lives, our marriage, and our finances to you. Regardless of the financial mistakes we have made in the past or the financial loss we may have incurred from previous relationships, cause us to recover all. Show us how to make the right financial decisions in our home so that every family member is abundantly provided for both now and in our future. Amen.

Things to ponder:

1. What financial challenges has your blended family encountered? How have you managed through them?

2. If you had it to do all over again, what financial decisions would you have made differently? Why?

3. Is there value in seeing a financial advisor to ensure your blended family's financial future is secure?

NOTES:

_____
_____
_____
_____
_____
_____
_____
_____
_____
_____
_____
_____
_____
_____
_____
_____
_____
_____
_____
_____
_____
_____
_____
_____
_____
_____
_____
_____
_____
_____

Establishing Authority in the Blended Family

"But if any provide not for his own, and especially for those of his own house, he hath denied the faith, and is worse than an infidel". – I Timothy 5:8

In today's society, there is so much misunderstanding of the authority that God has ordained for the home. Many Christian couples are experiencing strained marriages, over one-third of which are ending in divorce. Why? Could it be that they are not following the God-ordained authority which is meant to be honored and respected by husbands, wives and children? The establishment of God's authority in our lives brings about God's will in our lives and God's Word is very clear on the flow of authority that should be in every Christian home:

God is our first and foremost authority that must be respected. Second is the husband or father in the home, for he was given authority over his home along with the

"You have to think of you and your husband or wife as a team. You are working together to create a good measure of survival for the both of you, your kids, and everyone related to the family."

~Stan Dubin

responsibility for their well-being. Third is the mother's authority over her children.

God has set the husband as the delegated authority of Christ in the family and the wife as the representation of the Church. If the authoritative structure in the home is not recognized, then the plan of God for the family cannot be accomplished. This is true in a blended family as well. Remember we MUST follow God's design and order for the family. We cannot allow the composition our family to determine the structure and function of the family. The Word of God is the only standard for marriage.

It is important in the eyes of God for children respect and honor their parents, even if they do not agree with them. It is also the responsibility of parents to bring their children up in the ways of the Lord and in an atmosphere of love where they are nurtured and corrected in Christ-like love.

It is a proven fact that children who are products of divorce or separation, have a much more positive experience if all of the parents work together to ensure that the children feel loved and comfortable through the process. In a blended family the biological parent must do everything in their power to facilitate maintaining God's structure for the family. Their role is to bridge the gap between their biological children and the non-biological parent in the home so that God's order is not disrupted. It is your responsibility to explain to your children how the house is structured and how it will operate. It is your obligation to uphold your spouse's authority. You cannot allow your children to circumvent your spouse's authority; to do so will undermined his/her God-given position and reinforce your child's belief that they don't have to obey your spouse.

The non-biological parent must operate in God-given wisdom. You should spend the bulk of initial time together building trust and demonstrating genuine love and concern for the children in your new family. Keep in mind, more than likely you are viewed by the children as an "intruder" so their trust and proper response to you may take time.

It's always best if blended family issues are sorted out well before entering into that next marriage. Realistically though, very few people give it the time and attention that is truly required. If you haven't jumped the broom yet, ask yourself a few questions: If I'm the husband am I ready to take on the responsibility of someone else's children? Am I willing to care and provide for them like they are mine? Am I man enough to lead my wife and my children? If I'm the wife am I willing to follow my husband's lead? Am I willing to require that my children follow my husband's lead? Are there any items on the table where my children come before my spouse?

If you're already in a blended family, there may be some adjustments to be made in order to get back to God's pattern for marriage and the family. James 1:5 tells us if we lack wisdom in anything whatsoever, we can ask God and He will give it to us. Ask God today for the wisdom you need to order your family, and begin to experience the blessings that God promised will flow from the head.

Remember, Psalm 127:1 *"Except the LORD build the house, they labour in vain that build it: except the LORD keep the city, the watchman waketh but in vain."*

Let's pray...

Father, Thank you for the wisdom that we need to operate our family according to your order and structure. If we've functioned In any way outside of your plan, we ask you to reveal to us the way back to you. We desire your blessings, but we know that your blessings only come with your plan. Thank you for opening our eyes to see, and enabling us to do your will. Amen.

Things to ponder:

1. In what ways have you either upheld or undermined your spouse's authority? What was the outcome of your actions?

2. How can you prepare your children to accept your spouse's authority?

3. What is one valuable principle you learned from this chapter and how will you apply it to your blended family?

Cathy L. Wray

NOTES:

_____
_____
_____
_____
_____
_____
_____
_____
_____
_____
_____
_____
_____
_____
_____
_____
_____
_____
_____
_____
_____
_____
_____
_____
_____
_____
_____
_____
_____

When All Else Fails...
Keep Trusting God

God can't break His *word*. And because His *word* cannot change, the promise is likewise unchangeable. It's an unbreakable spiritual lifeline, reaching past all appearances right to the very presence of God. So let's do it-full of belief, confident that we're presentable inside and out. Let's keep a firm grip on the *promises* that keep us going. He always keeps His word. So let's walk right up to Him and get what He is so ready to give. Take the mercy, accept the help. Now, relax, everything's going to be all right; Rest, everything's coming together; open your hearts, love is on the way! -Excerpt from the books: Hebrews and Jude (MSG)

If you're like me, there've been times in your life when trusting God hasn't been easy. Perhaps that time is right now! Maybe your marriage isn't where you would like it to be. Perhaps it's far from ideal...even very far from being happy...and you've been praying and trusting God to turn things around. Your heart becomes established in trusting

"You have trusted Him in a few things, and He has not failed you. Trust Him now for everything, and see if He does not do for you exceeding abundantly above all that you could ever have asked or thought, not according to your power or capacity, but according to His own mighty power."

~Hannah Whitall Smith

God when you remember the faithfulness of God toward you on a daily basis. Meditate on the many times He has come through for you in the past when you could not see a way out. When you look back you'll see God has never failed you; even when things seemed like they were wrong for a time. It may have felt as though God had forgotten His promises, but in the end God will always prove faithful to you personally as He has throughout history. Have faith in God. God does do repeat performances! He is faithful! What He has done in your life once before He can do again. And that's a good reason to hold fast...to keep on believing...and to hold on today to the promise that God has put in your heart.

One of my favorite scriptures is Numbers 23:19, *"God is not a man, that he should lie; neither the son of man, that he should repent: hath he said, and shall he not do it? or hath he spoken, and shall he not make it good?"* This scripture defines the character of God in its simplest terms. God can't lie and won't fail. Since God cannot lie and He is unable to fail, I can have complete confidence that He will do whatever He has said to, and for me.

Not only is God incapable of failure, He knows about and cares about everything that we are facing and He wants to help us. Hebrews 4:15-16 assures us that there is grace available to help us in any situation that we may face. *"For we have not an high priest which cannot be touched with the feeling of our infirmities; but was in all points tempted like as we are, yet without sin. Let us therefore come boldly unto the throne of grace that we may obtain mercy, and find grace to help in time of need."* Everyone goes through difficult times. In fact there is nothing that you will face that someone else, somewhere else has not also encountered. So when you're being faced with tests and trials that seem to weigh you down just go to God. Boldly tell Him what you need and receive the mercy for your weakness and the grace that's there to help you.

Here are four powerful tips to strengthen your faith in God (Brown 2013):

o   Take no thought for your life (Matthew 6:25). When we take too much thought for our lives in the way of worry, it weighs us down. We are meant to be free of worry, reasoning, and stress, and the only way to be free of those things is to have faith in God.

o   Be anxious for nothing (Philippians 4:6). If you want to experience the fullness of the Father's best, you must believe in His ability to properly care of you.

o   Be still and know that He is God (Psalm 46:10). He is our Heavenly Father who cares for us. So, we don't have to worry, struggle to figure everything out, or even try to make things happen.

o   He will keep him in perfect peace whose mind is stayed on Him, because he trusts in Him" (Isaiah 26:3). Perfect peace can only be found in trusting in God. So the bottom line is to believe that He has your best interest in mind, and He has a good plan for your life (Jeremiah 29:11).

Let's Pray...

Father, Thank you for always being faithful and for never failing us. We know that we can trust you to keep your word, so help us to rest in your promise and trust that you will come through for us again. Amen.

Things to ponder:

1. Have you been anxious and worrisome about things your family may be facing? Write out a list of all the things that are challenging you and find the scripture that promises God's help for that situation.

NOTES:

_____

_____

_____

_____

_____

_____

_____

_____

_____

_____

_____

_____

_____

_____

_____

_____

_____

_____

_____

_____

_____

_____

_____

_____

_____

_____

_____

Holiday Joy

Even though holidays are intended to be joyous times of celebration with family and friends, they can often prove to be some of the most stressful of times for those of us in blended families. Arguments over who will get the kids, where they will open their gifts, and quite often competition between parents for who will purchase the best gifts, are issues that arise. Make a decision this year to keep peace in your home the way it was meant to be.

Some really good advice to remember is found in I Peter 3:10-11, *"For he that will love life, and see good days, let him refrain his tongue from evil, and his lips that they speak no guile: Let him eschew evil, and do good; let him seek peace, and ensue it."* You see, we will never be able to determine how everyone else will behave, but we can always be responsible for how we handle ourselves in situations that we are confronted with. In the blended family we have plenty of opportunities to allow the enemy to steal our joy...but choose not to let him! With that being said, no matter how hard you try, sometimes

"There is no ideal Christmas; only the one Christmas you decide to make as a reflection of your values, desires, affections, traditions."

~Bill McKibben

the other parties just won't cooperate. That's why Romans 12:18 tells us, *"If it be possible…live peaceably with all…."* When you simply are not able to, do your best and trust God for the rest.

You probably feel like you've already spent too much time bending over backwards to make things comfortable for everyone else. But, Galatians 6:9 admonishes us *"…be not weary in well-doing."* God always honors and rewards our faith, patience, and diligence. If you make one more sacrifice for the team it won't go unnoticed, you will be rewarded in due time. When it seems like you're always the one making the concessions, just keep taking the high road. My personal testimony is that it pays off in the end. Don't try to make the other parent look bad. Don't expose them, even if they're not doing their part. The kids will find out all they need to know in due time, but don't you be the one to take the devil's role of being the accuser. Proverbs 10:12 tells us that hateful acts stir up strife and contention, but the God-kind of love always covers.

Here are some helpful tips for keeping joy during your holidays:

o **Be Creative to Avoid Conflict** - If it's your ex's turn to have the kids for a holiday, start your own holiday tradition by celebrating at your house a few days earlier or a few days later. Make it a big hoopla for the kids so that they don't feel like they are missing or sacrificing, but rather gaining. Don't make the kids have to choose sides…ever.

o **Pursue Peace** - Romans 12:18 encourages us to keep on doing our part to create an atmosphere of peace. Psalm 34:14 tells us to look for ways to find peace. You won't necessarily be able to change how the other parties conduct themselves, but you can certainly clean your side of the street.

o **Do Unto Others What You Would Want Done to You** - Let's face it, you haven't made the all of the right decisions every time either. Make a commitment to follow the Golden Rule. If (when) you were the one acting out, how would you have wanted to be treated. Matthew 7:12 says, "Do to others whatever you would like them to do to you. This is **the essence** of all that is taught..." (NLT)

If you're a Believer, then Jesus is the real reason for all of our holiday seasons! So, don't let the stress and pressures that come with this time of year force you to behave in a way that doesn't represent Him. Keep joy in your home this Holiday!

Let's Pray...

Father, you are the God of peace and you promised to give us your peace. Give us your wisdom for the holidays this year. We take authority over all the power of the enemy, who would try to bring envy, bitterness, and strife. We make a determination to walk in your love and exhibit Christlikeness in all of our dealings. Amen.

Things to ponder:

1. Create a holiday tradition for your family that will de-stress your holidays this year. Make it a family effort.

2. In what way can you take the high road with your ex this year for the holidays?

3. You may not be able to control everything, but what are some ways that you will control you this year?

Cathy L. Wray

NOTES:

_____
_____
_____
_____
_____
_____
_____
_____
_____
_____
_____
_____
_____
_____
_____
_____
_____
_____
_____
_____
_____
_____
_____
_____
_____
_____
_____
_____

Your Blended Family is not Second-Rate

People who are in blended families are there because they've suffered some failure or some loss from a previous relationship, or married someone who did. Even though divorce and remarriage seems commonplace in our society, there is still a certain stigma that is associated with it that can leave you feeling like your family doesn't quite measure up. I've got great news for you - that's not how God sees you! *"The LORD preserveth the strangers; he relieveth the fatherless and widow"* (Psalm 146:9). He is the one who is setting the solitary into families. He's the one who is restoring the walls that were broken down. So, don't buy into the notion that your blended family is second rate.

I do want to reiterate however, that God is not the author of divorce. God is a god of covenant and God hates divorce. So if you've experienced divorce, it's a result of at least one of three things: 1) disobedience or deviation from God's plan in some way, 2) not being

"I can't change the direction the wind has blown, but I can adjust my sails to always reach my destination."

~Jimmy Dean

137

built up enough in the word to resist the attacks of the enemy, or 3) not waiting for God's timing or His best in a mate. Sometimes it's all three reasons (it was for me). The good news is that just like when Adam fell in the Garden of Eden, God has provided a way of redemption for us. When He redeems us He makes us brand new and puts us back on course for destiny.

Don't spend your days and nights agonizing over the past. What's done is done. Do make sure that you have reconciled where you failed in your previous relationships and are committed to doing it God's way this time. Ask God for the wisdom you need to move forward. Ask Holy Spirit to lead you and guide you into the truth you need for today. Stop believing that God's blessings don't extend to you...it's a lie from the enemy. God is ready to help you and ready to bless you; He simply wants us to turn to Him.

Here are some tips to help you keep the right perspective:

o   Begin to confess the Word over your marriage and family. Faith comes by hearing the Word. Keep telling yourself what God says about you, individually and as a family.
o   Lovingly correct people who try to make you feel unworthy.
o   Create family and marriage mission statements that give your family a framework for reaching your purpose.
o   Eliminate references that minimize your family's value and commitment to one another. Terms like 'step', 'his kids', and 'her kids' emphasize division rather oneness.

Let's Pray...

Father, help us to forget the things that are behind and reach toward the things that are ahead. Thank you for making us new and whole. Thank you that our marriage is not second-rate and that we're still eligible to fulfill your purpose for our lives. Amen.

Things to ponder:

1. Have you thought of your blended family as second rate? If so, how did those thoughts cause you to think less and expect less for your family?

2. Do other people's thoughts and reactions toward your family affect your family's esteem?

3. What steps will you employ to change your mindset and move into all that God has for you?

Cathy L. Wray

NOTES:

_____
_____
_____
_____
_____
_____
_____
_____
_____
_____
_____
_____
_____
_____
_____
_____
_____
_____
_____
_____
_____
_____
_____
_____
_____

God's Covenant Trumps Man's Arrangement

From Genesis to Revelations the bible shows us the character of God. One prevailing theme throughout scripture is that God is a God of Covenant. He is a covenant-making, covenant-keeping, covenant-revealing, and covenant-empowering God. God does nothing outside of His covenant, which is His Word.

The Covenant-Making God. God knew that there was not another person in the earth that was capable of fully keeping their side of the agreement. So, Hebrews 6:13 shows us His solution. He made a promise against His own integrity, "*For when God made promise to Abraham, because he could swear by no greater, he sware by himself.*"

The Covenant-Keeping God. Not only has God given us His Covenant, but He has every intention on keeping His promise to us. He's not like other people we interact with…He can never fail or fall short of his word. Deuteronomy 7:9 says, "Know therefore that the

"Marriage has a unique place because it speaks of an absolute faithfulness, a covenant between radically different persons, male and female; and so it echoes the absolute covenant of God with his chosen, a covenant between radically different partners."

~Rowan Williams

LORD thy God, he is God, the faithful God, which keepeth covenant and mercy with them that love him and keep his commandments to a thousand generations..." Another scripture says, *"My covenant will I not break, nor alter the thing that is gone out of my lips."* (Psalm 89:34)

The Covenant-Revealing God. We don't have to fret that we will never understand or apprehend to the promises, because God makes sure that we get it. He gives revelation knowledge into the true nature about everything and in every situation, if we will just ask Him. Psalm 25:14 says, *"The secret of the LORD is with them that fear him; and he will shew them his covenant.*

The Covenant-Empowering God. God is not finished yet; He doesn't just dangle His promises in our face like a carrot that can never be attained. He actually enables us to grab hold of the promise and make it a reality in our lives. Deuteronomy 8:18 assures us, *"But thou shalt remember the LORD thy God: for [it is] he that giveth thee power to get wealth, that he may establish his covenant which he sware unto thy fathers, as it is this day."*

Marriage is a vertical and horizontal covenant initiated and established by God himself for man. Vertical in that when two people enter into the marriage covenant they are saying to God that they are willing to uphold and fulfill their part of the covenant based on their relationship to Him for life. Horizontal in that individuals are saying to each other that they are willing to uphold and fulfill their part of the agreement for life!

In order for the marriage covenant to be established all parties must understand and fulfill their part of the covenant agreement. The marriage covenant is non-negotiable and cannot be altered...it's an "as is' agreement. Those entering into it cannot change it to fit it for your personal convenience. If we add to or take away from the marriage covenant it ceases to be a covenant and becomes an arrangement...God cannot bless man-made arrangements. If you're in a blended family today it is because either you or your spouse failed at keeping the covenant agreement in a previous marriage. Don't make the same mistake again. Make a commitment to operate in your marriage based on God's covenant requirements so that you can expect God's covenant blessing.

The mystery of becoming one is a part of the covenant that can only be experienced by a man and a woman who are married. Ephesians 5:31-32 says, *"For this cause shall a man leave his father and mother, and shall be joined unto his wife, and they two shall be one flesh. This is a great mystery..."* The word mystery here is the Greek word *'mustareon'* and it means that which can be made known only by divine revelation, and is made known in a manner and at a time appointed by God to those only who are illumined by His Spirit. Did you know it will take revelation knowledge to be married God's way?

Well, if you're starting over again or well into the game the second time around, you can make a determination that, beginning right now, you and your spouse will experience the mystery of the covenant of marriage. Get into the Word and get God's word for what you can expect this time. Based on His covenant, you should expect that God will be with you; that He will help you; that He will guide you; and He will cause you to come out on top. Don't settle for anything less than that, and don't let the devil convince you otherwise. Here are a few reminders of God's covenant promised concerning your marriage:

o **Victory:** "And the LORD shall make thee the head, and not the tail; and thou shalt be above only, and thou shalt not be beneath." – Deuteronomy 28:13
o **Power:** "Two should one chase a thousand, and two put ten thousand to flight..." – Deuteronomy 32:30
o **Unity:** "...a threefold cord is not quickly broken." – Ecclesiastes 4:12
o **Example of Christ:** "For this cause shall a man leave his father and mother, and shall be joined unto his wife, and

they two shall be one flesh. This is a great mystery: but I speak concerning Christ and the church."

Let's Pray...

Father, your word tells us that in you we can become one. It tells us, that when done your way, our marriage can be an example of Christ's love for the Church. Forgive us for deviating from your plan and put us back on course for experiencing your blessings for marriage. Amen.

Things to ponder:

1. What does the word covenant mean to you?

2. How does God's commitment to His word influence your commitment to your word?

3. What are some promises of God that you are expecting for your marriage and blended family?

NOTES:

_____

_____

_____

_____

_____

_____

_____

_____

_____

_____

_____

_____

_____

_____

_____

_____

_____

_____

_____

_____

_____

_____

_____

_____

_____

_____

_____

_____

Effective Communication

I read a funny story; it went something like this:

"A man feared his wife wasn't hearing as well as she used to and he thought she might need a hearing aid. Not quite sure how to approach her, he called the family doctor to discuss the problem. The doctor told him there is a simple informal test the husband could perform to give the doctor a better idea about her hearing loss. Here's what you do," said the doctor, "stand about 40 feet away from her, and in a normal conversational speaking tone see if she hears you. If not, go to 30 feet, then 20 feet, and so on until you get a response." That evening, the wife is in the kitchen cooking dinner, and he was in the den. He says to himself, "I'm about 40 feet away, let's see what happens." Then in a normal

> *"If there is any great secret of success in life, it lies in the ability to put yourself in the other person's place and to see things from his point of view as well as your own."*
>
> **~Henry Ford**

tone he asks, 'Honey, what's for dinner?" No response. So the husband moves to closer to the kitchen, about 30 feet from his wife and repeats, "Honey, what's for dinner?" There was still no response. Next he moves into the dining room where he is about 20 feet from his wife and asks, Honey, what's for dinner?" Again he gets no response so, He walks up to the kitchen door, about 10 feet away. "Honey, what's for dinner?" Again there is no response. So he walks right up behind her. "Honey, what's for dinner?" "Smith, for the FIFTH time I've said, CHICKEN!'"

Moral of the story: The problem may not always be with the other party as we may have thought. It could be very much with us instead! Someone once said that effective communication is to a marriage, what blood is to the body...marriage cannot survive without it.

The author and social scientist Leo Rosten said, "Behind the need to communicate is the need to share. Behind the need to share is the need to be understood." Given the unique nature of the blended family there will be many opportunities for mis-understanding. Hebrews 13:16 admonishes us about communication in this way, *"But to do good and to communicate forget not: for with such sacrifices God is well pleased."* The Greek word for communication in this scripture is the word *'koinonia'*. By definition it means the share or participation in fellowship, association, intercourse or intimacy that a person has with another. Koinonia is not casual agreement or the simple transmission of information, it is essentially the embodiment of the deepest levels of communication and covenant. I believe this is what God was referring to in Genesis 2:24 when He said *"...and they shall be one flesh."*

Effective communication begins with listening. Effective listening requires emotional investment. It means seeking to understand your spouse's emotions as much as what is being said with words. The good listener will almost always know how to respond appropriately because not only are they listening to their spouse but they are also listening to the Holy Spirit and he will lead and guide the listener to a solution even if not immediately.

To gauge whether you are communicating effectively with your spouse, I want to share these Five Levels of Communication:

1. **Cliché' Conversation** – This is where the conversation is surface and safe. We talk about the weather, our favorite color, or some casual event. At this level we stay safe behind our defenses.
2. **Reporting Facts About Others** – Here we talk about others and what they are doing or not doing. We're just reporting the facts at this stage; we are not offering any personal opinions or making a commitment on where we stand.
3. **Communicating Ideals and Judgments** – Here is where true communication really begins. Each person is willing to step out and risk telling their heart-felt opinions and judgments, which reveal their character and values.
4. **Communicating Feelings and Emotions** – at this level the person shares ideas and judgments. His/Her feelings underneath are revealed and the person starts to show who they really are. Effective communication in relationship begins at this level.
5. **Complete Emotional and Personal Communication** – All deep relationships get to this place and stay on a consistent basis. It is unrealistic to expect to stay at this level permanently since life is fluid and new issues arise that force us to start the communication cycle from the beginning.

Conflicts are going to arise in any relationship. Decide to just be married and work through your conflict. Don't destroy one another with your words, but rather seek to understand and build one another up. Here are some principles that can help as you work through sensitive issues:

o Focus on the problem and not the person. As you bring up issues, talk in a non-accusatory manner. It doesn't really matter who is right or wrong as much as how you handle yourself through the situation.
o Listen and ask for clarification to avoid misunderstanding.
o Make sure the goal of your communication is aimed at improving your marriage relationship. Communication in marriage should transcend communication with all others.
o Seek the good of your spouse. This should be your priority. Your spouse should always see and hear the love and affection you have for them, even when you're resolving conflict.

Let's Pray...

Father, you said that we would become one flesh in marriage. Help us to move past superficial, surface communication and experience koinonia in our marriage. Help us move past the fear of being vulnerable and truly let our guards down with my spouse and cause our communication to go far beyond any communication we have with any other human. Amen.

Things to ponder:

1. List the five levels of communication and describe what level you and your spouse currently relate on.

2. If you don't currently communicate on level 5, what factors hinder you?

3. What steps will you take to move you closer to level 5?

4. Examine your motives...do you communicate to share or to be heard? What is your rationale for the method you chose?

NOTES:

_____
_____
_____
_____
_____
_____
_____
_____
_____
_____
_____
_____
_____
_____
_____
_____
_____
_____
_____
_____
_____
_____
_____
_____
_____
_____
_____
_____
_____

Closing the Back Door: The Decision to Forgive

"Forgiveness is the only way
to break the cycle of blame
and pain in a relationship…
It does not settle all questions
of blame, justice and fairness…
But it does allow relationships to
start over. It is not our capacity
to think that makes us different,
but our capacity to repent, and
to forgive." ~ **Philip Yancey**

*"A happy marriage
is the union of two
good forgivers".*

~ Robert Quillen

Luke 17:1 quotes Jesus as saying, *"Then said he unto the disciples, It **is impossible** but that offences will come: but woe unto him, through whom they come!"* This scripture tells us that it is impossible that offenses will not come. In other words we will be offended from time to time. So someone will say or do something that we will not like and we will be offended as a result. But Luke also shows us that offence will have an affect on us, our marriage, and the health of our Christian life. So the question is not will we be offended the question is how we will handle the offence when it comes.

The word offence is translated from the Greek word *'skandalon'*, which is derived from our English word scandal. It means something that traps or ensnares and causes us to be drawn into sin. I remember hearing a story about people hunting monkey's in Africa. The documentary was very interesting because they explained that a monkey is a very intelligent animal and is almost impossible to catch. You basically have to set up a trap for it to catch itself. The tribes people would dig a hole in the ground where the monkeys could see it. Next they would take a shiny object and dangle it in sight of the monkeys. After they had gotten the monkey's attention they would put the object in the whole and hide behind a tree nearby and wait. Sure enough after a few minutes the monkey would come and stick his hand in the whole to get the object. The only problem is the whole would be big enough for the monkey's hand to enter into the whole but once he grabbed the object his hand would be too big to pull it out. Literally the tribes men would come and repeatedly beat the monkey with a stick until it was dead and the monkey would never let go of the object. The monkey was lured in by the trap, but refused to do what was necessary to become free from the snare.

God the Father has put on the inside of each one of us the unique capacity to forgive. We can simply refuse to hold onto hurts and wrongs done to us because we've been created to be like God. Romans 5:8 provides an excellent demonstration of how God has forgiven us: *"But God commendeth his love toward us, in that, while we were yet sinners, Christ died for us."* When we were actively against Him, He forgave us and sent His love toward us. When we refuse or are slow to forgive, it becomes an emotional trap that the enemy uses to eventually destroy us spiritually. Isn't interesting that Jesus said in Matthew 19:8, *"Moses because of the hardness of your hearts suffered you to put away your wives: but from the beginning it was not so."* In the beginning it was like that, but over time as we allow unforgiveness to set in, our hearts become hard and hardened hearts lead to divorce.

Unforgiveness not only affects us emotionally, it affects us physically. According to a study published by Hope College in 2001, indirect scientific evidence suggests that the health implications are directly related to our ability to forgive. Research connects blame, anger, hostility and other unforgiving responses like harboring a grudge and rehearsing hurts to health eroding diseases in the body, particularly heart disease. When we choose not to forgive, we open the door for the enemy to destroy our marriages, we hinder the effectiveness of our prayers, and we open ourselves to attacks on our physical health. God designed for married couples to be heirs of life together; He planned that every one of our prayer requests be answered; and He purposed for us to live our days in health and wholeness. Close the back door to the enemy by refusing to walk in unforgiveness.

A few pieces of advice when it comes to dealing with offense:

o   Being offended is a choice. When we are offended it is because we have chosen to become offended. We can choose or we can choose not to be…just decide that you will not be offended by the actions of your spouse.
o   The Bible tells us that it is impossible for offenses not to come. So we will be offended every once and a while. The idea is to not stay offended. Release it before it has opportunity to affect your physical health and destroy your marriage relationship.
o   Recognize the signs. When you are angry, hurt, ready to explode, etc. These are signs that you have been offended. Do not try to justify it. Identify it. Deal with it and forgive.
o   Don't look for things to fight about, but rather find at least one thing you can agree on

- o Give your spouse the space to be who they are and respond in their personality.
- o Let the Word of God be the final answer for every situation.

Let's Pray...

Father, you said in your word that if I do not forgive, I would not experience your forgiveness. Soften our heart so that we can let go of past hurt. Help us not to allow the trap of the enemy to draw us into the sin of unforgiveness. Teach us by the power of your Spirit, how to handle our emotions in a way that pleases you and safeguards our marriage. Amen.

Things to ponder:

1. On a scale of 1-10 (1 being the lowest) how apt are you to hold a grudge against your spouse?

2. Do you acknowledge when you've wronged another family member? Do you ask for forgiveness when you're wrong?

3. What kind of boundaries can you set-up for yourself so that you don't harbor unforgiveness?

NOTES:

_____

_____

_____

_____

_____

_____

_____

_____

_____

_____

_____

_____

_____

_____

_____

_____

_____

_____

_____

_____

_____

_____

_____

_____

_____

_____

Going the Extra Mile

"And whosoever shall compel thee to go a mile, go with him twain." - Matthew 5:41

The U.S. divorce rate is staggering but people still get married with the idea that marriage is a 50/50 venture. I think many couples enter into marriage with this 50/50 mindset, whether they actually realize it or not. At first glance it looks like a reasonable system: the husband and wife each give half, contributing their efforts, responsibilities, and needs so that they meet somewhere in the middle. He takes care of the trash and house repairs, she handles the dishes and the shopping. Or maybe she gets up early to make his breakfast before work, and he chips in with the kids to give her a break after work. The 50/50 split appeals to many couples because it seems fair, it's attractive because it makes the relationship appear equal. But the truth is no one ever really gives their half. We keep a tally of the "selfless" tasks we've done for our spouses but we are blind to the extra miles they have gone for us.

"Always do more than is required of you."

~George Patton

159

We begin demanding that they give their half, convinced that we deserve it. And instead of "meeting halfway" our giving becomes conditional: if he picks up his clothes on the floor like he's supposed to, then I will treat him with respect. If she comes home on time like she says she will, then I will take her out like she wanted. The problem with understanding marriage as a 50/50 arrangement is that it orients the success of a marriage on equality. The concept of compromise, of meeting halfway, is dictated by the value of equality, which is certainly an American value but not necessarily a biblical one. God never intended for a marriage to be the type of relationship where you only give to get. A marriage is supposed to based upon unconditional love where each person gives 100% regardless of how much effort the spouse puts in. Is that fair? Of course not, but true love isn't based upon fairness. It's based on both parties doing more than is required. Christ did not preach a gospel of equality, but a gospel of humility, surrender, and service, and the relational theatre where these virtues are primarily played out is marriage.

I read somewhere that someone said, "Once you get married you learn how selfish you really are." So many married people have the attitude that they'll only do their part if their spouse does theirs. This is even more true for people marrying for the second and third times. That attitude just won't work in the real world...not if you want to stay married. Renowned motivational speaker Zig Ziglar said, *"Many marriages would be better if the husband and the wife clearly understood that they are on the same side."* In marriage we're on the same team. We are to give our ALL and expect nothing in return. THAT IS LOVE! When each person in a marriage gives all that they can give, not holding back, not keeping score, but freely giving, then that is when everybody wins; we will have a marriage that is a blessing- not only to us as husband and wife, but to our entire household.

Every couple wants their 'happily ever after' but if you will truly have decades of life together, you have to throw away the score card. Instead of worrying about who is winning and who is losing the key is working together and giving your all. Make a decision today to go the extra mile. Here are some ways to start:

o   Work on small things I can do on a DAILY basis for my marriage.
o   Don't consider a marriage a 50-50 affair! Consider it a *100 percent* affair. The only way you can make a marriage work is to have both parties give a hundred percent every time.
o   Wake up saying: 'What can I do for him, or what can I do for her?" instead of saying "Am I getting what I need out of this?"

Let's Pray...

Father, I belong to You and everything within my day is a blessing that You have provided. Thank You for going the "Extra Mile" for me! Sometimes going that "Extra Mile" in marriage seems difficult but help me to look at every opportunity that I come across as an opportunity to go the "Extra Mile" for my spouse...to give my 100% every time. Amen.

Things to ponder:

1. What can you do today that will let your spouse know that you want to please them?

2. Describe what going the extra mile means to you.

3. What percent effort do you think you've given to your marriage so far? In what ways can you make that better?

NOTES:

_____
_____
_____
_____
_____
_____
_____
_____
_____
_____
_____
_____
_____
_____
_____
_____
_____
_____
_____
_____
_____
_____
_____
_____
_____
_____
_____
_____
_____
_____

You're not in this Alone: Employing the help of Holy Spirit

If it will be your last opportunity to get a point across to someone, you would probably want to choose your words very carefully to make sure they left a lasting impression in the minds of your listeners. In John 16:13, Jesus is speaking his last words to his disciples when he says, *"Howbeit when he, the Spirit of truth is come, he will guide you into all truth: for he shall not speak of himself; but whatsoever he shall hear, that shall he speak: and he will shew you things to come."* God knows what each one of us is dealing with. He knows our pressures, He knows our conflicts, and He has made provision for each and every one of them in the person of Holy Spirit.

The difficulty with marriage is not just that there are two separate, distinct personalities attempting to merge into one being, it's also that we have an enemy who hates any institution that comes from God and will do anything to sabotage its success. Not to worry though.

"God knows what each one of us is dealing with. He knows our pressures. He knows our conflicts. And He has made provision for each and every one of them. That provision is Himself in the person of the Holy Spirit, indwelling us and empowering us to respond rightly."

~Kay Arthur

Whatever state you find yourself in today, traditional family or blended family, I assure you it is no surprise to God. He is keenly aware that this is your second or maybe third marriage, or that your current marriage is literally dangling by a thread. You don't have to dread or be in despair, God had foresight enough to get us the help that we would need. You don't have to struggle aimlessly or fail yet another time; take advantage of the help that has been made available. Romans 8:26 says this, *"Likewise the Spirit also helpeth our infirmities: for we know not what we should pray for as we ought: but the Spirit itself maketh intercession for us with groanings which cannot be uttered."* The literal translation of the Holy Spirit's role in our lives is Comforter. The Greek word for comforter is *'parakletos'*, or one who is called along beside us to help us and to plead our cause. Holy Spirit was sent to the earth specifically to get down in the trenches with us and help us secure the victory in every battle. The comforter that Jesus gave does more than just provide a sympathetic hug during a difficult time. He actually embodies several different functions on our behalf. Let's take a look at what exactly that means for us as believers:

- o Holy Spirit the Advocate – Holy Spirit is our supporter, our promoter, our activist. When things don't look like they're in our favor, He is there to turn the tables. He campaigns for us and encourages us in our spirit man to keep moving forward.
- o Holy Spirit the Intercessor – Holy Spirit is our intermediate, our liaison, and our go-between. He works for our benefit, negotiating the terms of our contract. He makes sure we apprehend what belongs to us.
- o Holy Spirit the Assistant/Helper – Holy Spirit is our colleague, our partner, and our collaborator. He helps us in any way that we may be deficient. He fills in our gaps and makes sure we are always at our optimum for every situation.

o Holy Spirit the Leader/Guide – Holy Spirit is the conductor, the director, and the pilot. He attends with us at every event. He provides the instructions when our direction is obscure. He monitors our progress and makes sure that we stay the course.

o Holy Spirit who Reveals – Holy Spirit gives us inside information. He discloses and divulges private information. He exposes the attacks of the enemy and uncovers our escape route.

o Holy Spirit who Empowers – Holy Spirit endows us with the ability to walk in our God-given authority. He enforces our permission to act and enables us to transcend our opponents' forces.

If you're in a blended family, the active presence of Holy Spirit should mean good news for you! It means that even though statistics are against you, God is for you. If we simply allow Holy Spirit to do his job with and for us, we can never lose.

One more very important role of Holy Spirit in our lives and marriages is this…keeping us in the love of God. If you've been married for any length of time, you know full well the opportunities to get out of love. The problem with that is when we get out of love we also get out of faith because our faith only works by love. There is a way that we can always stay in the love of Christ toward our spouse, and that is by praying with the Holy Spirit. When situations and difficulties arise, let your first recourse be to pray. Jude 1:20-21 shows us exactly how Holy Spirit will help us, *"But ye, beloved, building up yourselves on your most holy faith, **praying in the Holy Ghost, Keep yourselves in the love of God…"*** When we pray with the Holy Spirit's guidance He will help us. If Him the opportunity to settle us, He will keep us in the love of God regardless of the situation. When we operate in the love of God we will always want God's result and not our own.

Let's Pray...

Father, thank you for the precious gift of Holy Spirit to help us, to lead us, and to fight with us. Forgive us for trying to make it on our own. Today we surrender to your power and your authority. We agree from this day forward, to cooperate with Holy Spirit in our marriage so that we can fully realize your results and become the example in marriage you intended for us to be. Amen.

Things to ponder:

1. In a shore paragraph describe what Holy Spirit's presence means to you.

2. What can you do to allow Holy Spirit more of an opportunity to work in your life and marriage?

NOTES:

_____

_____

_____

_____

_____

_____

_____

_____

_____

_____

_____

_____

_____

_____

_____

_____

_____

_____

_____

_____

_____

_____

_____

_____

_____

_____

_____

_____

Epilogue

When we married we vowed to love our spouse forever, but the marriage ended in divorce. Now you're married again, or contemplating re-marriage. If you're in a blended family or anticipating entering into one, the odds don't have to be against you.

I've personally encountered Christian leaders who have reluctantly confessed that they've thought differently about their members who have been divorced. For those of you who are Christians, admittedly the church and the Christian community should be more vocal and purposely involved when it comes to ministering to the blended family. Perhaps the reluctance is in having to deal with the divorce/separation issue, or maybe the issue is simply a matter of out-of-sight-out-of-mind. Just know this, pre-marital pregnancy, divorce, and separation come with their fair share of scars, but no scar is beyond what the Blood of Jesus can erase.

I'm happy to inform you that while God is not a proponent of divorce, He does understand that life and marriage may not have been kind to you...that you might not have won that particular battle, but that doesn't have to be the end of your story. There can be blessing and happiness in marriage and family the second (or third, or whatever time) around. But, only if you do it God's way can you expect to have God's results.

My husband and I believe that God is raising us up to be a voice in this generation for the blended family. He has made our family a success and allowed us the opportunity to speak into the lives of hundreds of blended families already. It is our prayer that this Perfect Blend Devotional will provide the opportunity to revisit topics that your blended family may face, as often as you need to. We trust that you'll find the comfort and encouragement that can only come from the Word of God as you read the pages. And, lastly we pray that you will not just be a reader, but that you'll put into practice the words on the pages, and that every member of your blended family would develop into everything, and fulfill every purpose that God had in mind for them before the world began.

Bibliography

Altenhofen, S., Sutherland, and K., Biringen, Z. (2010). Families experiencing divorce: Age at onset of overnight stays, conflict, and emotional availability as predictors of child attachment. *Journal of Divorce & Remarriage*, 51:3, p. 141-156. doi: 10.1080/10502551003597782.

Brown, Daniel N. (2013)
Trusting God – 4 Powerful Tips to Deepen Your Faith in God. www.SmartChristianLivingBlog.com

Gordon, Jon (2012)
10 Thoughts About Leadership. http://www.jongordon.com/blog/10-thoughts-about-leadership-3/#sthash.L1lTWFAn.dpuf

Kela, (2008)
Blended Family Discipline. *Today's Modern Family*. www.todaysmodernfamily.com/index.php/83

Patel, Sadiyya (2011)
Are Your Expectations For Marriage Realistic? *BellaOnline: The voice of Women*. www.bellaonline.com

Sayre, J.B., McCollum, E.E., and Spring, E.L. (2010). An outsider in my own home: Attachment injury in stepcouple relationships. *Journal of Marital & Family Therapy*, 36:4, p. 403-415. doi: 10.1111/j.1752-0606.2010.00218.x.

Shivee, (2011)
Divorce Devastates Children: Find Out How! *Pregnancy & Parenting*, p. 1
thefatherlessgeneration.wordpress.com/statistics

Biography

Cathy Wray, along with her husband Pastor Douglas Wray, has counseled hundreds of families and couples. Her passion for cultivating Christ centered-families shows in their 22 years of marriage and commitment to their own blended family.

Cathy is a powerful preacher and Bible teacher who delivers a practical 'you-can-make-it' message. She is a published author whose passion for marriage and family is displayed in the many articles she has penned for *Journeyors Magazine*, *The Michigan Chronicle Newspaper*, *Prayer & Praise Magazine,* and *Keeping Family First Magazine.*

Together, Cathy and her husband have co-hosted TCT Alive, a Total Christian Television (TCT) network broadcast reaching more than 4.5 billion viewers worldwide and have appeared as regular guests on The Joys of Oneness, also a TCT broadcast.

Cathy has a Bachelor's Degree in Human Resource Management from Spring Arbor University and is currently pursuing a Master's Degree in Marriage and Family Therapy from Liberty University. She is also licensed and ordained as a full gospel minister through Word of Faith International Christian Center, and currently resides with her husband in Houston, Texas where they recently founded and pastor Impact Church. Cathy founded The Perfect Blend Workshop to minister specifically to the needs of blended families. She is 'mom' to five adult children, and eight grandchildren.

80369980R00114

Made in the USA
Lexington, KY
01 February 2018